THE STORY OF BMW MOTOR CYCLES

ROBERT CROUCHER

THE STORY OF BMW MOTOR CYCLES

ROBERT CROUCHER

PSL Patrick Stephens, Cambridge

First published in 1982

British Library Cataloguing in Publication Data

Croucher, Robert M.
The story of BMW motor cycles.—(Motor cycles marque histories series)
1. BMW motorcycle—History
I. Title II. Series
629.2'275 TL448.B18

ISBN 0-85059-416-2

Photoset in 10 on 11 pt English Times by Manuset Limited, Baldock, Herts. Printed in Great Britain on 100 gsm Fineblade coated cartridge, and bound, by Woolnough Bookbinding, Wellingborough, Northants, for the publishers Patrick Stephens Limited, Bar Hill, Cambridge CB3 8EL, England.

Contents

Foreword

The story of BMW motor cycles is not an easy one to tell. The length and familiarity of the story could so easily become a dead compilation of complex detail about transient names and passing dates. Neither is the task made simpler by writing from one country about events which mainly took place in another country, and another language. Like all histories it is an interpretation coloured by the realities of research and the perceptiveness of its sources. The BMW company has been witness to momentous events over a period of 60 years and the research difficulty is not what is available, but what must be left out. The problems of access and translation make balance difficult and force a distinctively British bias. Nevertheless, a determined effort has been made to enrich the events by clothing them in first-hand experience wherever possible. This book's claim to freshness comes from setting the well-known story against the memories of some of the people who were there and helped in its making. It is a collection of historical record, anecdote, reflection and commentary. It would be presumptuous to claim that it is definitive but it is hoped that it will awaken interest, challenge and inform opinion and give genuine reading pleasure.

Robert Croucher
Stapleford Abbots
Essex, 1982.

Introduction

Generations of bikers have come to agree that BMW motor cycles are probably the best in the world and that to own one is to experience the ultimate pleasures of two-wheeled transport. This respect and admiration has lasted now for almost 60 years, making the German built machines a living legend. This book has been written to explain how the legend began and why its fascination continues.

Because the technical side of BMW is already well-documented, this book is as much about people and organisation as machines. It pays tribute to the vital role that record-breakers and racers, designers and mechanics and sellers and buyers have played in building and extending this continuing story. It is a story with many unusual twists and turns. A pioneering company in the somewhat sophisticated area of aero-engine development finds itself reluctantly caught up in the simple and straight-forward business of hand-built motor cycles. It quickly hits on a winning design and then, despite the difficult financial times, diversifies into cars which establish an international reputation for the flair of their engineering. Despite a massive reversal created by the world at war, the company bounces back, unaided, to claim a position as one of the world's most exclusive vehicle manufacturers. Sometimes the stars of the story have been the bikes while, at other times, the cars have been in the ascendancy. This book concentrates on motor cycles but, on occasion, it makes sense to take the wider view.

The theme which constantly emerges is that to make or to sell or to ride a BMW motor cycle is a privilege not to be missed. Over the years great motor cycles have appeared and then declined into extinction, but the BMW label has had remarkable staying powers able, regularly, to adapt itself to new and different biking challenges. The BMW story may read like a legend but it is certainly not a myth. For successive model refinements have freshened the concept and launched a new band of devotees. The wonder of the story is not the preservation of the motor cycle inheritance, but the fact of a continuing contribution to biking technology and riding pleasure. It is a story which has not yet ended and the longer it continues, the better the re-telling becomes.

Acknowledgements

One of the pleasures in researching this book has been meeting and talking with so many people wrapped up in the enjoyment of BMW motor cycles. Contacts have been made with the present BMW organisation and with many people who have served in the past to bring the pleasure of the BMW marque to the biking public. Because of the time-lapse between events and their recollection, memories have sometimes failed and dates become confused but, invariably, the trail has doubled back to produce another piece to the jigsaw. Everywhere I met unfailing kindness and co-operation. My acknowledgements are listed in the order in which I met the people concerned and make no special distinction of value or relevance.

Invaluable help came from: BMW (GB) Ltd, where Grahame Pearce (Marketing), Alberto Criscuolo (Technical), Arthur Dalziel (Field Sales), Gordon Maggs (Public Authorities), Don Sibley (Parts), Merryl Rollason (Promotions), Les Glassock (Training) and Pat Myers (MD Motor Cycles Division) co-operated magnificently. BMW AG Munich, where Thomas Fuhrmann (Press) was a sensitive and lively mentor in Germany and Hans Fleischmann (BMW Archivist) helped with early photographs. Heino Würfel (Marketing) and Reinhard Emmer (Advertising) were informative at BMW Motorrad GmbH and Jutta Brückner was a charming guide in Spandau, Berlin. Back in England Ron Slater, his mechanics and Roger Measor at Hughenden M40, took an interest in the book and I was welcomed at several other BMW dealers—Bill Slocombe at Neasden, George White at Swindon, Alan Gurdon at Ongar Motorcycles and Vincent Davey at Gus Kuhn Motors. Racing memories were supplied by Jock West and Georg Meier, and David Willcox, Force Transport Officer of the Thames Valley Police, helped with Chapter 4. For information about BMW during the '70s Richard Styer, once of TKM and now with Colt Cars, was an inspired source. AFN Ltd, through Don Aldington, his nephew John Aldington and Lawrence Hardwick provided much useful information about BMW's famous pre-war concession and some insights into the post-war scene came from Charles Lock, now in Australia, and Alf Cook still working for MLG. George Saunders and Fred Secker of the BMW Owners Club were useful contacts and my perspective was widened by overseas contacts with Ralph Walker of the Marusho/Lilac Owners Club, Arlington (VA), (USA), the Turners (BMW Club, Victoria, Australia), Václav Hamsik (Czechoslovakia), Serge Chartrain (France), Simon Croucher (Italy) and George Brackins Edgewood (MA), (USA). Inspiration to keep going came from enthusiasts such as Frank Cox, Markhouse Motor Cycles, and veterans such as Fred Horton, still touring Europe at 75 on his R75 outfit, and Bob Hutcheon buying a new BMW in his seventies. Valuable help with photographs was provided by Martin Pover of Havering Technical College and Chris Kitts, a mechanic at Ongar Motor Cycles. Some of my problems with German were resolved by colleague, Hilary Wood. The back numbers of *Motor Cycle Weekly* and *Motor Cycle News* were useful points of reference, and starting guidelines were established by those who had trodden the path before—mainly L.J.K. Setright with *Bahnstormer* and Heinz Hartel's *BMW Motorrader*. Always in the background providing support and encouragement when the going got tough was my wife, Marjorie.

The BMW Story in brief

1896 The Fahrzeugfabrik Eisenach AG is opened by Heinrich Ehrhard making bicycles and electric vehicles.

1900 The Eisenach factory is making Decauville cars under licence from France. The car is called a Wartburg after the local castle.

1910 November 9 Georg Meier is born in Mühldorf.

1911 Gustav Otto, son of Nikolaus August Otto, creator of the Otto-Cycle, opens an aircraft factory on Lerchenauerstrasse at the eastern end of Munich's Oberwiesenfeld Airport.

1913 The Rapp Motorenwerke GmbH is established by Karl Rapp and begins production of aero engines.

1914 The Eisenach factory is busy producing military trucks.

1916 Karl Rapp and Max Friz found the Bayerische Flugzeugwerke AG and make aircraft engines as part of the German war effort. The engines are used in fighter 'planes including those of the squadron commanded by the legendary Freiherr Manfred von Richthofen.

1917 BFW produce their 500th engine and join forces with the Gustav Otto Flugmaschinenfabrik to become the Bayerische Motoren Werke GmbH.

1918 On August 13 the present company is formed, BMW AG. The number of employees is 3,500 and stock capital is 12 million Reichsmarks. A principal shareholder is a Viennese Banker, Camillo Castiglioni, and the managing director is Karl Popp, an Austrian naval officer with considerable experience of aero engine development.

1919 BMW has developed a high-altitude, six-cylinder aero engine developing 250 hp, but the Treaty of Versailles requires all production to be halted. This does not stop Franze Diemer using the Mk IV engine to set a world record climb to 9,760 m in June. To keep the company going BMW begins production of railway air brakes, farm machinery and castings for other manufacturers.

The R37 (BMW).

1920 BMW produces a 45/60 hp truck engine which also has marine applications. Development starts on a lightweight, two-stroke moped with a 148 cc engine which is marketed as the Flink.

1921 BMW begins production of the Bayern-Kleinmotor or type M2B15. This twin-cylinder motor develops 6.5 hp and is sold as a proprietary engine to the Victoria Company of Munich and several other smaller manufacturers of motor cycles in Germany. Much of the production capacity is devoted to air brake equipment and a major shareholding is now held by the Knorr-Bremse AG. At the old Otto-werke production is started of the Flottweg light motor cycles. The Fahrzeugfabrik Eisenach is taken over by Gothaer Waggonfabrik AG, railway rolling stock manufacturers.

1922 BMW markets its own flat-twin motor cycle, the Helios. The engine is installed fore and aft and not across the frame. BMW buys the factory of the Bayerische Flugzeugwerke AG on Lerchenauerstrasse for 75 million RM.

1923 BMW starts production of the R32 and exhibits the new model at the Paris Motor Show.

1924 Aircraft engine production restrictions are relaxed and work begins on a six-cylinder, 310 hp engine. The second series R32 motor cycle has improved front braking. The company now employs 1,200.

1925 The R39 250 cc model is introduced and the R37, an ohv racing 500, features in the nine-model line up. BMW motor cycles win over a hundred races this year including the German GP. BMW aero engines now hold 28 world records for speed, range, altitude and non-stop flight.

1926 Turnover has now reached 9 million RM. Research director, Rudolf Schleicher wins a gold medal in the International Six Days Event held on the Isle of Man. The Mk VI, a 12-cylinder, V-aero engine is produced; it is to become BMW's most successful liquid-cooled model. It remains in production until 1939. The first racing superchargers or *kompressors* appear on the motor cycle circuits.

1927 The Eisenach factory is taken over by the Shapiro company and starts the manufacture of Austin 7 cars under licence. BMW's turnover is now 17 million RM and there are now 1,500 employees. The first BMW 750 cc motor cycle, the 18 hp R62, appears. Total motor cycle sales to date are 25,000.

1928 BMW acquires the Eisenach factory for 2.2 million RM. BMW now involves itself in car manufacture and the first vehicle is the two-seater

Dixi, a BMW version of the British Austin 7 known as 'the flea'. The payroll now numbers 2,630. The first ohv 750 cc motor cycle is put into production, the R63. BMW acquires a licence to build American Pratt & Whitney air-cooled aero engines.

1929 Increased car production creates financial difficulties for BMW. The number of employees has now climbed to 3,860. Ernst Henne breaks a number of motor cycle speed records at the Avus track in Berlin and on the autobahn near Munich. With Paul Köppen he wins the gruelling Targa Florio race in Sicily. The pressed steel frames appear on motor cycles with the 750 cc R11. Total German annual production of motor cycles is 195,686 machines and BMW output amounts to about 5 per cent of this.

1930 Aircraft engines are selling well to Russia and Japan and the 1,000th Mk VI is delivered. The world is in a deep economic depression and Germany has enormous inflation and severe unemployment. Production begins of a utility 198 cc machine which takes advantage of tax-free ownership, and its riders do not have to take the stiff German driving test. The BMW 3/15 car wins in the 750 cc class at the Monte Carlo Rally.

1931 Strict cash flow limits just keep the company ticking over. The labour force remains static at 3,930 and bank debts of 4 million RM are re-paid. A BMW-engined Dornier Wal covers 27,300 miles (44,000 km) around the world in 234 flying hours. BMW motor cycles set up seven new world speed records pushing the sidecar record to 118 mph (190.83 km/h). Production of a four-cylinder, 20 hp car commences.

1932 Turnover at 19 million RM is the lowest since 1928. The labour force totals 2,800 workers. The German Army agrees to buy the 400 cc R4 model. Vehicle licence tax on motor cycles is suspended and there is a boom in sales. Henne pushes the 750 cc world record to almost 152 mph (244.39 km/h) at Tat in Hungary. The AM4, the first BMW-designed car, enters series production. The famous '30s airliner, the BMW-engined Ju 52, begins service life.

1933 BMW begins a series of ISDE wins by taking the major award in the Welsh competition. Turnover leaps to 32 million RM and the workforce now totals 4,720. The six-cylinder 303 sedan appears with the famous kidney-shaped radiator grill. It is the year Adolf Hitler seizes power in Germany.

1934 Turnover 82 million RM and payroll 12,576. Considerable investment in Munich and Eisenach to expand aero engine production. Ernst Henne again breaks the world speed record (246.049 km/h). The works riders on R4 machines again win gold medals at the ISDE held in Garmisch-Partenkirchen.

1935 The R12 is launched, the most popular pre-war model manufactured. It features modern style

Above *The R63* (BMW)
Below *The R11* (BMW)

telehydraulic forks, the first fitted to a series production motor cycle. On the autobahn outside Frankfurt, Henne pushes the land speed record to nearly 160 mph (256.046 km/h). Turnover reaches almost 128 million RM and the workforce is 11,113. AFN Ltd handle motor cycle imports to Britain as official BMW concessionaires.

1936 October 12, Henne using a streamlined 500 cc supercharged BMW reaches just over 169 mph (272 km/h). BMW wins a major contract to supply its 1,500 hp radial engine for the Reich Luftfahrtministerium. The type 326 car, with a 2-litre, six-cylinder engine and independent front wheel suspension, appears. This was the most successful car of the '30s and its styling influence continued after the Second World War. A military equipment division is set up at Eisenach to manufacture lightweight field guns.

1937 The type 328 car is announced capable of 145km/h and producing 80 bhp. The total of employees is now 14,000 and turnover reaches 143 million RM. Henne takes the world record at 174 mph (279.503 km/h) which is to remain unbroken for 14 years. In Ireland works rider, Jock West, wins the Ulster GP on a blown BMW racer. The Flottweg factory in Munich is taken over.

1938 The 100,000th BMW motor cycle rolls off the production line. Total annual production of motor cycles in Germany is now 327,580 and BMW account for about 10 per cent of this. The new model R51 has plunger rear springing. Aboard the *kompressors* West wins again at Ulster and Georg Meier becomes European Champion. A 328 team wins the famous Mille

The 328 Sport (BMW).

Miglia race in Italy. Turnover is 180 million RM; payroll is 18,624.

1939 Turnover leaps to 275 million RM and the workforce increases to 26,919. Meier and West come first and second in the Isle of Man TT race. Meier is the first foreign rider to win the prestigious Senior Trophy. War halts all production of civilian-use vehicles. Extra aero engine production is brought into use at Brandenburg.

1940 Production is started of the R75 military sidecar unit, which begins to equip whole motor cycle battalions in North Africa and on the Eastern Front. BMW again wins the Mille Miglia road race. For five years now the BMW sports cars have dominated the European race tracks. Number of employees tops 30,000. The BMW 801 engine is fitted to the Focke-Wulf 190 giving it a top speed of 660 km/h.

1941 Payroll reaches 35,419 and turnover is reported as 385 million RM. The last BMW side-valve motor cycle, the R71, ceases production. Preparation commences for series production of the BMW 109-003 jet engine.

1942 In January Karl Popp, BMW's first managing director, is retired from the company. BMW now employs 47,346.

1943 The first mass-production ever of a turbo-jet engine for aircraft begins. On March 10 the first bombing of the Munich factories occurs.

1944 Bombing of the factories takes place again on June 13 and July 11. The number of BMW employees is now 30,400.

1945 About a third of the BMW facilities in Munich have been destroyed by the Allied bombing. The American forces take Munich and many of BMW's machine tools in the Allach factory are confiscated. These include the special high-altitude engine test rig which had escaped the bombing destruction. Eisenach is occupied by Soviet forces. By September limited peace-time production of cooking utensils, wood planing equipment and bicycle parts begins. It is proposed to rename the production facilities the Bayerische Erzeugnungswerke, the Bavarian Production Works!

1946 The Russian-occupied Eisenach plant begins limited production of R35 motor cycles. The Munich plants service American military vehicles and produce household and bakery equipment. Permission is granted to build 100 R23s and 21,000 bicycles. The workforce amounts to 1,800. The total output of motor cycles from German factories is put at 1,445 machines. Georg Meier lifts BMW spirits by running the *kompressors* again and winning races.

1947 Meier forms the Veritas team and becomes national road champion on his BMW.

1948 BMW is allowed to produce vehicles again and exhibits a single-cylinder R24 at the Geneva Motor Show.

1949 Using engine blocks and parts which survived the war, BMW put together 9,450 assorted bikes. 'Schorsch' Meier opens a BMW dealership in Munich.

1950 The first post-war twin appears, the R51/2. Production increases to 17,000 machines and includes the R25 with rear wheel springing. Exports begin again to the USA and Britain.

The R71 (BMW).

German motor cycle manufacture at 29,900 units is almost back to pre-war levels.

1951 The R51/3 appears and a heavy-duty 600 cc model, the R67, starts production. New BMW motor cycles are again selling in Britain. At the Frankfurt Motor Show BMW presents its first post-war car, the 501. Only one hand-made model is available for customers to see!

1952 The R68 (the 100 mph bike) appears, claimed as the fastest German motor cycle in production. About 20 per cent of the production of twin-engined motor cycles are now exported to over 30 countries.

1953 Post-war sales of bikes reach 100,000. The R25/3 appears with new telehydraulic forks. Annual output of motor cycles reaches 29,000 but sales of the bigger bikes show signs of slump.

1954 BMW struggles with its marketing strategy. At

The R51/2 (BMW).

one extreme it offers the expensive eight-cylinder 503 car and for the popular market it is selling the Isetta bubble car. This town transport is powered by a motor cycle engine and is built under licence from the Italian Iso company. On the race tracks the 500 Rennsport begins a devastating domination of world sidecar competition which will bring the World Championship to BMW 19 times in succession. BMW currently holds 24 of the possible 27 world records in the motor cycle combination class.

1955 The R26 appears with fully-enclosed cardan shaft drive and full suspension frame. The R50, a machine popular with the police forces, starts production. The all-pivot frame of the RS racers is now fitted to every model and the new bikes feature Earles-type front forks which become a BMW fashion for 12 years.

1956-1958 Motor cycle sales remain poor. Production in 1956 is down to 15,500 and by 1957 only 5,400 bikes leave the BMW production lines. The BMW 600, a stretched version of the Isetta bubble car, is not successful. Talks begin of a merger with one or more of the competitors, such as Daimler-Benz, Zündapp or the Glas concern at Dingolfing. In 1957 Steib stop production of their famous side-cars.

1959 The year of crisis for BMW AG. The Annual Report closes in the red. Shareholders, led by Dr Herbert Quandt, rescue the company and it regains the confidence of the banks. The BMW 700 appears and proves to be an exceptional sports car success and puts BMW back on the road to profitability. The Allach aero engine facilities are sold to Man Turbo GmbH. Turnover is down to 117 million marks and the labour force numbers 6,000.

1960 The touring motor cycle models receive a boost in power with the S versions. The R27, the final BMW single, begins a seven-year production run. The R69 models feature a hydraulic steering damper.

1961 MLG Ltd use a factory-prepared R69S to establish new 12- and 24-hour endurance records at the Montlhéry circuit near Paris.

1962-1963 Motor cycle production is unspectacular at about 7,000 units a year. The R69S proves a successful production racer and long-distance endurance machine.

1964 BMW profits come from the highly-successful Michelotti-styled 1500, 1600 and 1800 series cars, the 'New Range'. Managing director, Karl-Heinz Sonne, introduces cost effective management practices throughout the company to improve efficiency. A massive re-investment programme is launched. Hans Gunther von der Marwitz joins BMW from Porsche to develop the next generation of motor cycles.

1965 By the end of 1965 turnover has reached 593 million DM and the workforce is 12,000.

1966 BMW buys sports car manufacturers, Hans Glas GmbH of Dingolfing. The machine tools and production facilities are shipped to South Africa to establish a BMW facility there. BMW Australia Pty Ltd is incorporated and a small assembly operation is started in Uruguay.

1967 BMW South Africa Invest Pty Ltd is created in Pretoria.

1968 Construction begins of a central spares facility at Dingolfing. Helmut Dahne starts to attract

The R69 (BMW).

attention as one of the few solo riders to be racing BMWs in modern times.

1969 Annual car production is 145,000 units. Turnover tops 1,537 million DM. The Stroke 5 series is launched. The BMW motor cycle frame is now two-piece with telescopic forks up front. The lightweight frame design with electric start is clearly influenced by USA market requirements, and is no longer suitable for sidecar use. Motor cycle production is shifted completely to Spandau, Berlin. Output there is about 30 machines a day. The move is required to make production facilities available at Munich for the expanding car output. Motor cycle production bottoms out at 4,700 units. The 'Schorsch' Meier company becomes part of BMW.

1970 Production of two-wheelers climbs dramatically as the new series breaks into the superbike competition. End of year output is 12,287 units. An ultra-modern car factory, capable of producing 350 units a day, is opened at Dingolfing. Construction begins on a high-speed proving ground at Ascheim. Turnover is 1,724 million DM.

1971 Turnover reaches 1,900 million DM. BMW now employ 23,000 workers. The production of 185,252 vehicles includes 18,772 motor cycles. BMW Kredit GmbH is started in Frankfurt.

1972 The new headquarters tower, overlooking the Munich Olympic Games site, is opened. BMW Motorsport GmbH is set up to organise BMW's wide involvement in car racing. BMW France is started to act as an importing company. Motor cycle production is 21,122 and the 500,000th BMW bike leaves the production lines.

1973 The Stroke 6 models appear with new five-speed gearboxes. BMW drops the 500 cc category and top of the range now includes three 900 cc models. The R90S features the new Hans Muth-designed bikini fairing which becomes a trend-setter. Motor cycle production is 20,856. Wholly-owned subsidiaries are set up in Belgium, Italy and North America.

1974 80 per cent of the world's Formula 2 cars are using the BMW 2-litre engine which develops 275 bhp. Only 3 per cent of BMW's racing budget now goes to motor cycles and that is concentrated in sidecars and off-road events in the hands of experts such as Sebastian Nachtmann. Bike production is 23,160.

1975 The BMW Holding Company AG is formed in Zürich. Motor cycle production is 25,566 and car output, with the popular six-cylinders back in production, reaches 221,298 units. Spandau makes its 100,000th motor cycle. Turnover is 3,254 million DM.

1976 The Stroke 7 series appears and it now includes the new generation of 1-litre motor cycle engines. The R100RS features a revolutionary, wind-tunnel tested fairing. Motor cycle production reaches 28,209. The separate motor cycle and marine engine divisions of BMW are created and BMW Schweiz AG is formed.

BMW AG, Munich (Author).

1977 Peak motor cycle production of the 1970s reaches 31,231 which is at the limit for the aged Spandau factory. BMW Austria GmbH is established.

1978 Car production leaps to 320,853 units but bike output falls back to 29,580. The model range is increased by the introduction of the R45 and R65 compacts. BMW management reaffirms that the motor cycle side of the business is important and will be expanded. Agreement is made with the Steyr-Puch company to develop lightweight diesel engines.

1979 BMW Nederland NV is formed. Turnover reaches 6,560 million DM.

1980 In September the R80 G/S dual-purpose machine

The R65LS (BMW).

heralds some dramatic styling changes in BMW bikes. The colourful machine features monolever rear suspension. Turnover is 6,898 million DM and a production total of 370,000 vehicles includes 341,031 cars. The dream car of the year is the M1 which produces 277 bhp and is capable of over 160 mph (262 km/h). One of these cars receives an unusual paint job treatment from artist, Andy Warhol. BMW(GB) is created and BMW now export two out of three of its motor cycle production. Total number of employees worldwide is 43,241 of which 37,246 are directly employed by BMW AG. Turnover of this international effort exceeds 7,000 million DM.

1981 The new Series 5 car is launched. The aerodynamic R65LS takes the old boxer concept to new styling heights. Extra production facilities at Spandau are completed and will be used for the next generation of BMW bikes. Responsibility for motor cycle research and development reverts to BMW AG. The production rate at Spandau through the 1970s is about 145 units daily. This could now be almost doubled. BMW take over its Japanese concession.

1982 The story continues with the motor cycling world anxiously awaiting firm news about the next generation of BMW bikes, coded the K589, and said to be in-line fours. Rumours from Ascheim also talk of the possibility of a 550 cc model putting BMW back on the motor cycle turbocharging scene again.

1

The concept is created

It seems strange that, so far as the early history of the motor cycle is concerned, BMW was not one of the pioneers. Indeed, by the time the company appeared as a serious motor cycle manufacturer, the world's bikers already had the choice of more than 70 of what were to prove the most famous names in the business. At the start of the '20s, sometimes described as the golden age of the motor cycle, the keen rider could select from a range which went right through the alphabet from ABCs to Harleys, Nortons, Scotts and Zündapps or any number of limited production marques. Yet now, 60 years on, many of those pioneer machines are only memories or museum pieces. Few have had the staying power of BMW which, after a late start, continues to prosper. Moreover, the present models still trace a direct ancestry to the original design of Dr Max Friz, the firm's first bike maker.

Birth of a concept, the R32 (BMW).

In the world of biking the name BMW has become identified with the flat twin engine layout, integral with gearbox and shaft drive of Friz's first blueprint. The long development life of this design has been confirmation of its inspired creativeness and efficiency. Its continued effectiveness is all the more remarkable when it is considered how much bikes and biking have changed since those early days.

The birth of the BMW boxer concept is traditionally dated to the presentation of the R32 model at the 1923 Paris Motor Show. It was success at last after several years of abortive attempts to produce a marketable machine for the boom in powered two-wheelers. Had Friz been any less of a perfectionist the BMW label might have been attached to a short-lived, two-stroke lightweight or a heavy and uncompetitive in-line flat twin. Indeed, things had been so difficult for the company since the end of the Great War, that BMW might easily have become a name associated with railway braking systems rather than motor cycles and cars. The R32 was to change all that and its launch coincided with a long-term settlement of BMW's early parentage issues.

The setting for the story of BMW motor cycles began to take shape on March 7 1916 when two of Munich's small aircraft factories amalgamated to form the Bayerische Flugzeugwerke AG. It was wartime and the merger brought together the Rapp Motorenwerke which had been making aero engines since 1913 and the Gustav Otto Flugmotorenfabrik, which specialised in biplane construction. The new company concentrated on engine production in the Rapp plant at the eastern end of the Oberwiesenfeld airport in Munich. The directors were Karl Rapp and Dr Ing E. Max Friz. Their engines were soon attracting attention because they were fitted in some of Germany's front line fighter planes, including those of the renowned Richthofen squadron. The German High Command had developed a new and powerful weapon in the aeroplane and suitable engines were in great demand. Just across the border from Munich, the Austrian Navy was keen to obtain additional aero engine production facilities for its air force. Thus it was that Franz Josef Popp, a naval engineer on detachment with the Austro-Daimler aero engine company, brought his own special talents and Austrian money to BFW AG. On July 29 1917 the Bayerische Motoren Werke GmbH came into existence. Popp became its managing director, a post he was to hold until 1942. A year later the company went public with a share of capital of 12 million RM and a workforce of 3,500. One of its new directors was Fritz Neumeyer who was later to establish the rival Zündapp motor cycle works in Nuremberg.

By now the Great War was in its final phase. In the east the revolution and Lenin had taken Russia out of the war but the decisive event, the United States joining the conflict, had already occurred and Germany faced a disastrous defeat. The future for BMW looked decidedly uncertain. The signing of the Treaty of Versailles and the disarmament of Germany should have brought the production of aero engines to a total halt. Yet, even as the victors were assembling in the Galeries des Glaces at Versailles, Max Friz was supervising the installation of a water-cooled, six-cylinder 300 hp in-line engine to a DFW biplane at the BMW factory. Following secret tests this plane, piloted by Zeno Diemer, climbed in 89 minutes to a then world record height of just over 30,000 ft (9,760 m). This flight on June 17 1919 was a sensational achievement and resulted in the Allied Commission of Control confiscating all plans and documents relating to it.

These were difficult times financially and inflation was such that a litre of petrol cost over 150 RM. For a while raw material stocks for aircraft production were turned into tool boxes, agricultural implements and office furniture. Producing castings for other companies led to a contract to produce parts for railway braking systems. An attempt to get back into engine manufacture led to an 8-litre engine which could be used in lorries, buses and for marine purposes. This Friz design was a 45/60 hp water-cooled four and was called the Bayernmotor. It was to be followed by the first steps into motor cycle production.

The first BMW motor cycle was an assembly operation on what today would be called a moped. It was a 148 cc two-stroke single and was named the Flink to suggest a nimble and lively performance. It used a proprietary Kurier engine designed by Curt Hanfland. The Flink was not successful for BMW but it inspired the sale of the old Gustav Otto works in 1921 to produce the Flottweg range of motorised cycles. Friz meanwhile was developing a new bike engine, the type M2B15, which became known as the Bayern-Kleinmotor. This was a twin-cylinder, side-valve engine of 493 cc and produced 6.5 hp. At first this engine was sold to other motor cycle manufacturers such as Bison in Austria, Heller and SMW in Germany and, in particular to the Victoria Werke in Nuremberg. Victoria, one of the more successful German motor cycle manufacturers, had started in 1886 as bicycle makers. The BMW engines were fitted to Victoria machines at the Sedlbauer factory in Munich. Much later Victoria became part of the Zweirad-Union when it was merged with DKW and Express in 1958. The versatile Bavarian light engine was also used by the Mauser armaments company to power a three-wheeler car called the Einspurwagen.

Still, however, the main output from the BMW factory was air brake equipment for trains. From 1921 BMW was as good as owned by its main contractor, Knorr-Bremsen AG of Berlin. The

Right *The BFW Flink* (BMW).

Below *BMW Kleinmotor fitted to a Victoria motor cycle* (BMW).

turning point had, however, been reached and the disorganisation caused by the post-war controls was about to fall into place. In 1922 BMW increased its stock capital to 120 million RM and acquired the BFW property on Lerchenauerstrasse. Here part of the factory was partitioned off and the company turned seriously to motor cycle production. The outcome was the Helios, named after the Greek sun god. It used the horizontally-opposed twin M2B15 engine but it was fitted lengthwise rather than across the frame. With its chain drive, its heavy frame, spindly-looking brakes and laid-back handlebars it was a typical product of the times. On the road the Helios proved to be unsatisfactory. Friz, still prevented from following his true profession, aero engine design, took a fresh look at the motor cycle and came up with a winner. The result was a more powerful and sophisticated engine coupled to a dependable drive system. The concept had at last been realised and this innovative design was to father all subsequent BMW bikes down to the present.

The BMW R32 was a seminal design for the German motor cycle industry. It featured a horizontally-opposed engine set across a duplex tubular frame and linked directly with the gearbox. A three-speed, car-type clutch and gearbox drove the rear wheel through a propeller shaft with a fully-floating axle. At a stroke the design solved many of the problems which plagued motor cycling in the early days—particularly overheating and unreliable drive systems. The solution was so successful that BMW have continued to employ these features on their bikes ever since.

The flat engine configuration exposed the cylinders to the passing air stream and created very efficient engine cooling. The horizontally-opposed layout gave almost perfect balance and delivered smooth low-down torque with a minimum of engine vibration. The compact engine was low slung in a strong frame and this helped to give the machine very good handling characteristics. The shaft drive made the rider forget about the chain and belt troubles which affected most other bikes of the time. Shaft drive also simplified rear wheel changing and this was a considerable bonus at a time when the state of the roads and the quality of motor cycle tyres made punctures a frequent occurrence. Maintenance in general was simplified because access to the plugs, ignition, valve gear and carburettors did not require any time-consuming removal of parts. Made as it was by 'plane makers, the R32 had a reliable and sturdy feel about it. By comparison with much of the opposition it was a quality product.

Individually none of these design features was especially original. It has remained a matter of continual debate amongst some motor cycle enthusiasts as to how much this BMW design had in common with current models of the time. Certainly, the R32 resembles the 398 cc ABC flat twin which appeared at the London Olympia Show in 1919. Interestingly, this bike, designed by Granville Bradshaw and produced by the Sopwith Aviation Co, was advertised as 'The World's Best Motor Cycle'. Horizontally-opposed twins were almost the fashion for the 1921 models. This cylinder layout had featured on the Douglas bikes used for despatch riding in the Great War and even before that Joseph F. Barter had used the system in 1905 for his Fairy twin. Shaft drive

The Helios motor cycle (BMW).

The R32 (BMW).

systems had been in use as early as 1903 on the Belgian FN (Fabrique national d'Arme de Guerre) motor cycles and in 1922 the Vauxhall Car Co had shown a unit construction, four-cylinder, in-line machine with shaft drive. The secret of the R32's appeal, however, was the blend of distinctive features with excellent engineering.

Design is frequently a question of re-discovering what has been tried before, improving it and announcing an innovation. Friz created his masterpiece by employing the best ideas then around and putting them into production. As a one-off, the R32 would have been an interesting design of the times, but in reliable production it created the BMW concept of motor cycling. Biking, always exciting, could now also be a pleasure.

3,100 R32s were to be produced over the next three years from a remarkably well-organised assembly line in a corner of the aero engine works. Although braking and suspension fell somewhat short of the ideal and the low compression, side-valve engine lacked power by comparison with some of the contemporary models, the home market found this elegant design an extremely desirable machine. Many of the riders buying them were still used to bikes with unreliable belt-drive, noisy and vibrating engines, rigid frames and the feeble carbide lighting. For them, the R32 represented an ultra modern concept in biking.

In 1924 Max Friz was able to return to aircraft engine design following the lifting of restrictions on German aero engine production. He had, however, already set in train the development work which was to build on his basic concept. In 1924 Franz Bieber won the German road racing championship on a modified R32 and BMW sporting victories really took off with the arrival of the overhead-valve M2B36. Race-bred development was to become a feature of BMW's motor cycle manufacture and from the beginning many of the design engineers were serious biking people. Research director Rudolf Schleicher not only specially prepared the racing R37 but he rode it successfully in the 1926 International Six Days Event held in England. This victory gave BMW useful overseas publicity and drew the world's attention to the products of the Munich factory.

The R37 had the shortest production run of any BMW model but its new engine was twice as powerful as the original side-valve version. Ten special racers were prepared featuring a shorter wheelbase and a novel light-alloy cylinder head. They were successful in over 90 races in 1926 and one, with Paul Köppen on board, won the German grand prix.

Between 1923 and 1929 Germany quickly regained its pre-war prosperity. Things improved dramatically after 1925 when France finally conceded the Ruhr. BMW grew, keeping pace with the steady demand for its quality machines. A range of nine models, all based on the developing BMW legend of safety, distinction and total reliability, were now available. The line up included the R39, the firm's first quarter-litre single. At first sight this looked like a rejection of the basic Friz concept, but it created the precedent for the compact BMW. Although a single cannot be as smooth and balanced as a flat twin, in every other sense the bike looked like and acted like a BMW. It had the typical clean unit-design engine with a light-alloy housing for the overhead valve gear, cardan drive transmission, the sturdy black frame with its elegant white-lining, heavy-duty mudguards, balloon tyres and footboards. The big model had been descaled without compromising established priorities. Subsequently, circumstances forced BMW several times into the smaller bike market but, whenever this happened, the machine always looked the high quality part even if the performance did not quite match expectations.

By 1927 BMW had produced its 25,000th motor cycle and its first 750 cc bike, the R62, was ready to be launched. The popularity of sidecar touring meant that models such as the R52 and R57 were fitted with chair mountings as standard equipment. More surprisingly perhaps, headlights were only available as special accessories! These '20s superbikes set fresh standards with their powerful but quiet magnetic 'Novotex' drive. It was becoming clear, however, that the new rich were looking beyond motor cycles to the status and comfort of the car.

On November 14 1928 BMW took over the Dixi factory in Eisenach and began producing two-seater Austin 7 cars under licence from England. This tiny 15 hp saloon sparked BMW's interest and experience in car manufacture. It was a small beginning for what was later to dominate the company's activities, but that is another story. This move to diversify did, however, have important implications for the biking side of the business. One immediate effect was to experiment with an entirely new frame technology presumably influenced by the newly-acquired car body tooling. BMW bikes after 1929 featured the pressed steel 'Star' frames.

These elegant-looking machines were extremely strong and remained in production for five years. The R11 side-valve and the R16 sports version ran to five model changes each. It was a clear example of the BMW tradition of deliberate step by step improvement. Changes included the introduction of twin carburettors which, in 1932, boosted the output of the R16 by a third and the replacement of the long gear-shift lever by a stubby gate-type change located on the tank. The R11 and R16 models set new standards of sophistication for BMW motor cycles. They were sold at an on-the-road price which included lights, horn and speedometer which on many other bikes were still being considered as extras. Unfortunately, they appeared on the market when the boom times in Germany and the rest of the world were ending.

Once more the story switches to survival and it was the steady bike sales which kept BMW going when all around them companies were toppling. The firm was particularly vulnerable because of its substantial investment into four-wheelers at a time which coincided with a general world recession and the economic collapse of the last years of the Weimar Republic. In 1931 17,000 German companies went bankrupt, but BMW was able to keep in production by clever financial management and the diversity of its manufactures. In 1931, with the crisis at its worst, the utility R2 motor cycle sold for 975 RM compared with the 1,630 RM for the R11 and the 2,500 RM which would purchase a BMW car. Interestingly, the company had introduced a deferred payments scheme as an aid to sales in 1929, which anticipated the no-interest inducements of recent years.

Within two years the Third Reich had been established and BMW was through to smoother waters. The company's diversification now really began to pay dividends. In the air BMW-powered aeroplanes were breaking speed and endurance records to all parts of the world. BMW engines were fitted to the JU 52 then the most reliable and successful passenger-carrying airliner flying. In 1934 substantial aero engine building capacity was created at Eisenach to meet heavy orders from Russia and Japan. On rail a 12-cylinder BMW engine had been used to drive an experimental airscrew train to a world speed record of 143 mph (230 km/h). On the rash of new autobahns spreading across Germany it became possible to appreciate the value of six-cylinder motoring with

Above *The 250 cc R39* (BMW).

Below *The R16 ohv sports 750 cc* (BMW).

The tax-free R2 machine (BMW).

the new 303 series cars. On the motor cycle side of the business things were also looking good, helped by the success and reliability of the bikes in virtually every form of sport and endurance event. The gloss and prestige came in particular from the amazing triumphs of the supercharged machines which had been dominating race and record tracks in Europe for over a decade.

By the middle of the '30s the opportunity to own and ride a BMW motor cycle was being taken not only by German and continental enthusiasts, but by riders as far afield as the Dutch East Indies and Australia. Early road reports in the biking Press were often lyrical in praise of these R32 derivatives. They catered for all the needs of the biking public. At the bottom of the range was the utility R2 which was BMW's tax-free model. This 198 cc machine even came in three-wheeler form for parcel carrying and in Germany no licence was required to ride it. The sturdy R4 proved to have such good off-road capability that it was ordered in numbers for the German Army. The R11 tourer was about to be replaced by the enormously popular R12 whose sales were to average 9,000 a year over a four-year production run. Often these bikes were fitted with sidecars using either the Steib or the Munich-based Royal chair. A number were converted to commercial use working the German mails or equipped for local fire fighting. For those wanting a hotter type of engine there were the R16 and R17 sports machines, both of which featured in the export trade.

By 1935 the original R32 had spawned over 30 different models all clearly stamped with the BMW look and characteristics. Rigorously engineered and built with high-quality components BMWs represented unashamed elitism designed to give the motor cyclist problem-free use and the guarantee of sheer riding pleasure at all times. It could be seen in the immaculate finish to parts such as crankcase castings and the clever design details which simplified maintenance and ensured long life and reliability. Compared with the other models of the time, the BMW range were frequently described as being without vices and offering a smooth, turbine-like ride which would induce little rider fatigue even after a long period of continuous riding. Invariably, it was only the heavy car-type clutch and gearbox that came in for any substantial criticism. This was the stuff of the concept. It was how the legendary image was created.

Building the image

Max Friz, chief design engineer at BMW from 1916 to 1945 (BMW).

Max Friz, the architect of BMW's first motor cycles, was foremost an aviation specialist and only engaged in bike design as a result of unplanned circumstances. The bikes were made in a factory with a workforce which had already proved itself highly professional in the manufacture of aircraft components. This clearly helped create the initial image of fine engineering which grew so quickly around the early bikes. Friz and the BMW workers were motivated by the standards and values of the planemakers. Flying has always demanded fail/safe engineering of the highest quality in order to succeed in getting heavier than air materials into the skies and then to convince the user that the risk of them dropping back to earth is minimal. Against such standards, the unsophisticated road machines of the 1920s were positively crude and unpredictable. Thus the R32 made the world look up when it first appeared in the autumn of 1923. The product was instantly recognised as superior and an improvement on what had gone before. With touching modesty and just a hint of national pride, a report in *Motor Cycling* described the R32 as similar to an ABC, looking like a Douglas from the front and comparable in finish to the finest British machines currently available! Clearly, given the right sort of marketing, success was assured.

Few other motor cycles in the world have as consistently been compared with the very best as BMWs. Bikers recognise many classic motor cycles in the two-wheel hall of fame such as the Hendersons, the early Indians, the two-stroke Scotts, the BSA Goldies, the Norton racers and the Vincents, but none can claim to have survived for so long at the top as the BMW flat twins. Certainly there have been exceptional models such as the 1926 Brough Superiors which were even labelled the 'Rolls-Royce of motor cycles' in an effort to describe their qualities, but these have been the few which flowered and then faded from the scene. For BMWs the claims go on. One measure of their standard has been the extent to which BMW copies have been reproduced at various times in France, the USA, Japan and the Soviet Union.

Cynics counter by suggesting that such claims have not always been warranted and the motor cycles have sometimes been over-rated and certainly over-priced. Yet, it must be obvious that no product, least of all a motor cycle, could survive at the top so long on misleading or arrogant advertising. Bikers are not noted for their gullibility and they are normally quite clear about what they admire. For most riders BMWs have always stood at the prestigious end of the market and have been something to aim for. Indeed, the challenge of ownership has helped perpetuate the image and preserve the tradition.

A visitor to any BMW establishment, whether it be the head office, the marketing company or a dealer invariably takes away one consistent impression that BMW people have pride and faith in their products. There is sometimes an intensity about this feeling which can be awesome, but it is also catching. Even in the muddy archive photographs of the old bike factory at 76 Lerchenauerstrasse, Munich, there is a confidence about the workers and their orderly production line. Today this conviction is still actively spread by the highly professional marketing people within the BMW organisation. The promotion of BMW's image is treated very seriously through careful advertising, exhibitions and sponsorship.

One of the most significant aids to image-building for BMW has been the white and blue trademark which was brilliantly conceived in 1916. The emblem represents a stylised rotating propeller against a bright blue sky. This not only aptly symbolises the company's beginnings, but it also incorporates the traditional local colours of Bavaria. For BMW workers this logo stands to remind them that the priorities of aircraft construction, particularly quality, safety and reliability, should also be applied to all other company products. For the motoring public 60 years of consistent use have created a familiar sign that is instantly recognised and respected. For in today's marketing jargon it has become an essential part of the corporate identity and it is to be seen featured on dealer's frontages, publicity material, clothing and accessories as well as the vehicles themselves.

The production line of the R32 at the Oberwiesenfeld factory, Munich (BMW).

Right *BMW advertising. Leave the routine of the week, the car and the working clothes and ride away to freedom.*

The image of freedom and power created by Patrick Litchfield.

The R80 G/S offers anywhere biking!

Exclusivity helps to promote an image and, although there are more BMWs registered now than ever before, they will never become as commonplace as the ubiquitous 'Hondukawas' of the Japanese manufacturers. The Big 4 in Japan are geared up to produce more machines in a week than BMW could turn out in three years! The traditional, hand-crafted production methods used to create BMW motor cycles limit output and make them expensive. BMW machines have always been rarities on the road, in the air and at sea. A 1931 British road test of the R16 published in *Motor Cycling* described vividly how the machine was a centre of interest for policemen on point duty, bus drivers and small boys whenever it was stopped. Sixty years of production have only put about 850,000 BMW motor cycles on to the world's roads and their attention-grabbing qualities have hardly been diminished. Owners today experience that same awed reaction whenever they park from passers-by keen to know what sort of speed it will do, how big the engine is and, invariably, how much it costs. Indeed, the author was actually stopped by a Thames Valley police patrol simply to let the officers get a closer look at the finish on an R100RT. That this sort of situation should exist is, of course, what years of image-building have been about. BMW owners know that they have either bought the best that money can buy or, at least, they have spent as much as it is reasonable to spend in order to indulge biking dreams. Greater affluence and world-wide trading have made BMWs more widely available, but older dealers remember when a deposit on a BMW was only the start of ownership, and possession might take a further four months of waiting for delivery. Such deferred gratification is only practised by people for the most desirable of wants.

From time to time the company have tested the success of their image-building and, in 1935, published a list of world opinions. Even allowing for careful editing they suggested a wide measure of agreement that BMW motor cycles were seen as in a class of their own in satisfying so many different biking purposes in such different environments. Half a century later BMW have again been carrying out a worldwide image survey to find out just what makes people choose their bikes. In Britain this survey was organised by Marketing Direction Ltd and reported in January 1981. Their survey by postal questionnaire revealed a number of unique dimensions about the people who buy and ride these motor cycles. Similar surveys have also been carried out in Germany and other world markets and the information gained is being used by BMW for forward planning of their sales strategy.

In Britain the survey certainly confirmed that the BMW image is known and appreciated. The typical British owner was found to be aged 36, male and, if riding the RS or RT models, definitely from the up-market end of the social spectrum. What professional advertisers like to describe as 'the affluent, grey-haired teenagers'. The survey also revealed that BMW owners have had a longer full-time education than the average British male. This perhaps justifies a long-standing BMW practice of up-market advertising aimed at the successful and often using long, technical explanations or clever playing on words. A trick of language was employed in creating the label 'Meistershaft' and a 1975 advertising campaign described the R69 as 'Scene not herd'. Given an intellectual market, the advertising can be aimed at the thinking buyer who wants to know about the product rather than be sold illusions. This is not, of course, to suggest that BMWs cannot be sold by shameless appeals to sex or snobbery. Adverts for the R90s claimed it would out accelerate a Maserati Bora and much of the mid-'70s advertising clearly identified the motor cycles with power, prestige, performance and possession.

On machine usage the Image Surveys show that the most popular use is for week-end touring. Typical annual use amounts to 8,000 miles in Britain and 12,000 km in Germany. The younger owners do rather more as they are more likely to use their bikes for everyday commuting. In this respect Britain differs from most other countries where big bike riding is invariably seen now as a leisure activity. Nearly three-quarters of BMW owners also have a car and, for the older person, the bike is normally a hobby vehicle and secondary to the car. For BMW this evokes the image of the company man relaxing at the week-end and able to enjoy the freedom of two-wheel mobility in the open countryside. On the other hand, the enthusiast may see a caricature of the typical BMW owner standing by a highly polished RS, fitted with every conceivable extra, which only emerges on dry, summer Sundays. His face glows from contact with real air, the adrenalin flow and slightly advanced blood pressure and his racing style leathers hang somewhat baggily, stretched by good-living and the onset of middle age. Contemptuously, they are sometimes dismissed as poseurs or the vertical riders.

Heading the reasons why people buy BMW motor cycles is their legendary reputation for reliability and high quality construction. These are characteristics which the company has worked consistently hard to achieve and account for the open hostility to copies or any attempt to fit non-standard parts to their machines. A desire to maintain total quality control means that the guarantee with a BMW is always based on the use of genuine spares and servicing through officially-recognised agencies. A consistent element of all BMW advertising has been the claim that each model is the culmination of carefully planned and evaluated product development. It is a proud boast that things change on BMWs only if they can be show clearly to improve quality or performance. As the advertisments have it—'When something is right it should never be changed, only improved'. Critics often rage at this arrogance, and a disgruntled owner can always be produced to catalogue a list of faults on a rogue machine. Yet the longevity and reliability of these machines have been demonstrated time and again since the very first models took to the roads and the tracks.

When the BMW image was being forged, sporting achievement played a considerable part in establishing the name. The record-breaking activities and racing successes of the 'blown twins' in the 1920s and '30s identified BMW with the world's best. For 20 years after the Second World War the company was still active in motor cycle sport. Recently these activities have been much restricted, even though the firm is still heavily committed to motorsport as a means of promoting car sales. Part of the explanation is BMW's reluctance to be associated with failures which could dent its image. Riders and sponsors have not always found BMW keen to support motor cycle sport or record-breaking attempts unless there are pretty firm guarantees that they will succeed. Racing is a high-risk business with considerable prestige going to the winners, but the two-stroke domination of the race tracks since the '70s has effectively curtailed BMW's involvement in motor cycle sport except where four-stroke endurance can be put to good use. At present such activity is devoted almost entirely to off-road, enduro events.

One of the company's most successful racing collaborations was with the German rider, Mike Krauser. He raced dirt-track in the USA and in Europe is best known for organising the BMW works sidecar team in its final effort to take on the two-stroke machines in 1976. The beautiful-looking outfit with a fuel-injected, four-valve Rennsport engine was not, in fact, a winner, but it helped establish the name of Krauser with BMW. Most BMW owners have come to associate Krauser with officially-approved panniers and other accessories, but his company also enjoys the support of BMW for the production of very smart cafe-type racers.

For the past decade BMW has been a world company and its powers to control and influence its image overseas have grown considerably. Although its daughter companies have independent responsibility for making their operation pay, the influence of the parent company is clear to see in advertising and promotional activities. Close links by telex and computer make it easy to spread ideas around the wider company. Munich head-office has become an efficient data-gathering centre on the riding characteristics and buying habits of motor cyclists in every country in which BMWs are sold. The Munich advertising department designs promotional material and creates the display stands for the various international motor cycle exhibitions where the firm is represented. These stands invariably have a high technology theme and are built of top quality materials appropriate to BMW's international image. At the 1981 UK Motor Cycle Show in Birmingham the symbolism of advanced technology was softened somewhat by the addition of a pretty girl and a Bavarian oompa-pa band. Munich-inspired advertising is used in most European countries, but in Britain, the USA and Australia the importing companies often tailor their own campaigns to local market conditions. Not only are the German advertisements found rather heavy on the technical information side, but sometimes the translations are rather daunting. A recent example stated 'BMW motor cycles are excellent for planned undertakings'—a rather dead-end experience which could hardly have been intended!

The BMW stand at the 1980 Cologne Motor Cycle Show.

Above and above right *The Krauser BMW with greatly altered frame geometry* (Krauser).

An important function for all the importing companies is to ensure that the white and blue quadrant is before the public eye as often as possible. To this end public relations agencies are employed to get the message across. Advertising is normally found in all the biking journals and sometimes appears in coffee-table type magazines such as *Punch* and *Playboy* in order to attract the uncommitted. Test reports in the motor cycle journals are an important publicity vehicle and importing companies keep a fleet of demonstrators for Press evaluation purposes. Times change, models alter, but the message of biking journalists about BMW machines has remained firm and positive for over half a century.

'If it were only for the rare distinction of having held the world's motor cycle speed record . . . the BMW would be one of the most talked-about motor cycles of today. But when there are combined in its design more features of the kind widely recognised as 'advanced', than in almost any other machine, it is not hard to understand the worldwide fame which it has achieved.'

Thus begins the test report on the R16 in the March 18 1931 edition of *Motor Cycling*. It goes on to describe the 'extraordinary cleanliness of design', the carburettor giving 'smashing acceleration and also a hyper-silky tick-over', the brakes being 'all that brakes should be' and concludes that, 'the BMW should fulfil the tastes of those with an appreciation of the admiration of the outside world. A wonderful machine'. Later a 1939 road report on the R23 ohv single praises its good riding comfort and goes on to describe the bike 'as the quietest single in production'. A 1955 test report on the R69 becomes almost poetic as it describes the bike 'gliding with the grace of a Rolls-Royce', possessing a riding position which fitted 'as unobtrusively as a Saville Row suit' and so quiet that it 'whispered' with scarce a sound except 'the rustle of cleft air'. Truly, it concludes 'a machine to keep ahead of the great motor cycle renaissance'. One of the more recent succinct type of report simply records the characteristics of the R65 as: 'Best features: Smooth, reliable high-speed cruising. Handling. Simple DIY Maintenance. Riding position. Brakes. Headlight. Ancillary equipment. Worst features: Price.'

A spring 1981 *Which Bike?* report on the R100CS and R100RT praises the '81 models as 'the best the factory has ever made' and goes on to describe the Bavarian twins as the 'yardsticks for other manufacturers to work at matching'.

Extra publicity can also be gained from various promotional activities such as road shows by dealers or major sports events like the Isle of Man TT races. For the 1981 UK Milk Race BMW provided a fleet of bikes for marshalling duties. The BMW Rideaway has been a marketing feature since 1977. Dealers are flown to Munich personally to pick up new demonstrator machines which are then ridden back across Europe in convoy. This mass movement of brand new BMWs has frequently attracted the attention of the media, apart from being good for fostering company/dealer relationships through a shared experience. It has not, however, been an event without problems. A customs misunderstanding at the French/German border on the UK 1981 Rideaway almost ended in a diplomatic incident. A long delay and a heavy fine resulted in the dealers on limited-edition black and gold R100CS machines having to make an indignified scramble to the coast to catch the last ferry back to Dover.

BMW recognise that their dealers are an extension of the company and as such play a key role in promoting its image. Every satisfied customer is an ambassador for the company and equally a disgruntled owner can damage their reputation. Being in the front line, dealers clearly must give unrivalled service and be positively committed to BMW values. To help in this the importing companies support dealers in local promotions and advertising and back dealers in any ways which further the aims of BMW.

The maintenance of the image does not, of course, lie solely in the hands of the company. At various times the image has been affected by world events and the general economic situation in a way which is beyond company control. Sometimes it is simply a question of the BMW image becoming too exclusive as a consequence of unfavourable exchange rates. Then BMW motor cycles become too expensive and sales dive, as they did in the USA at the end of the '70s. An interesting example of temporary sales resistance which was eventually overcome, occurred in Britain at the start of the '70s when the superbike revival really got going. The big bike image then was to do with 'scratching', the hard riding which wears the rubber of the foot rests and tries to get grass stains on the toe caps. Riders, used to the traditional Bonnie or the new breeds of Japanese superbike feared that the huge, extending cylinder heads of the BMW would ground on the first bend. Resistance was overcome by offering free test rides, a novelty in the trade then, and advertisments claimed that, contrary to popular opinion, a BMW can be leaned at an angle of 52 degrees which is beyond the maximum angle given in the rules for racing bikes. Fortunately, this disclaimer was used before slicks and other ground effects aids came into use but, in any case, it was soon found that it takes some pretty hairy riding to cause one of the pots to ground. Certainly, BMW(GB) never had to deal with a claim resulting from such an accident.

Other circumstances have been more earth-shattering, such as the Second World War. This was a colossal set back for BMW which had been riding high at the close of the '30s with advanced models such as the R5 and R51 selling well at home and abroad, and international prestige being gained from road racing and record breaking. War was to isolate BMW from the international scene, damage its markets and set back its development plans because of destruction at the factories and the appropriation of many of its machine tools by the victorious Allies. Not until the Geneva Show of 1948 were there signs that the image was to be reborn. Once again the company's reputation rested on the back of a motor cycle, even though it was the atypical R24 single. Still that was preferable to a situation

British dealers on the Hans Muth Limited Edition R100S between Madrid and Santander, Spain, in the 1980 BMW Rideaway (Two Wheeler Dealer).

where BMW almost stood for rare vehicles, cooking pots and bicycle trailers. Cheekily others cashed in on some of the old BMW reputation.

The Soviet zone of Germany re-opened the Eisenach factory which had not been bombed and which during the war had been the main production facility for BMW motor cycles, and began manufacture of a bike based on the old R35 design. The famous R75 *Wehrmacht maschine* with its 26 hp 750 cc ohv engine and sidecar disappeared into the Soviet Union to emerge later from the Minsk motor cycle works as the Ural and Dnieper outfits. In France CMR bikes were created from war surplus R12 and R71 machines, while on the car side the Bristol project got under way in Britain using BMW 328 engines and development plans. BMW was able to preserve some of its dignity by persuading the East Germans to distinguish their output by switching to the white and red quartered EMW badge. Through the '50s the BMW recovery was slow and uncertain and towards the end of that decade the company was nearly sold off to its rivals. Perhaps it was the sleeping image of past glories which finally persuaded the shareholders to rally to its support.

The North Africa Korps version of the R75 with a later Dnieper MT10 look-alike from the USSR (Phil Brunsdon).

Since that trough in its fortunes the company has climbed back to the top as a world brand leader. Today, however, the fortunes of the motor cycle side of the business clearly rest on the phenomenal profitability of the cars. That this still cannot lead to complacency has been demonstrated recently by the problems experienced in restoring the motor cycle reputation in the USA where the run down in the Butler & Smith concession created a substantial cut-back in sales. Satisfying a world market is a complicated operation with such intense competition from the mass-market side of the business. It is made challenging because varying driving conditions and standards of living in different parts of the world mean there are a number of perceptions of the BMW image. In the USA the BMW bike is much loved in its older model forms because they are so different from the traditional laid-back Harleys and because they are such classic bikes to restore for trailoring to Daytona and the rallies for veteran machines. the new models tend to be used as summer runabouts for professional and service people.

In Europe price and taxation laws complicate the market. Despite the Common Market, BMWs are considerably cheaper in Germany than elsewhere. In Denmark extra taxes on an R45 treble its factory price which means that riders have to be exceptionally dedicated to run one in preference to the cheaper, mass-produced models. The price advantage and the licensing regulations in Germany mean that the R45 can be a first-time purchase for young riders. Whereas in France a difficult driving test, the high cost of insurance and a 33 per cent sales tax make the big *moto* a toy of the rich and the smart. In Italy riders traditionally go for the cafe-racer models of which there are many famous local makes. The good looks and the sporting feel of the RS has made it popular and recently the BMW range has been in demand for its tourers and off-road machines especially in the better-off north. By contrast, the BMW image in Australia has tended to be associated with the 'drifters', young people who work for half the year and then spend time wandering their continent's open spaces or heading for Europe and the 20th century version of the Grand Tour. The BMW's reliability and long-range are major selling points for such adventure trips. Typically, Australian advertising for these bikes features the open desert, the escape route to the big country.

These differences may alter the patterns of sales, but the overall BMW image still manages to emerge. It is neatly summed up in a 1980s advertisment which said, 'What makes every BMW motor cycle the same, is what makes every motor cycle different'. BMW motor cycles do stand in a class on their own.

The image of BMW riding pleasure in the early '60s Freude am Fahren *by Isetta Bubble Car and R60* (AFN LTD—the W.H. Aldington collection).

3

The ultimate riding machine

The expression 'the ultimate riding machine' was first applied in the USA to the R90S, BMW's 1973 flagship. At other times the range has been more modestly described as 'probably the best bikes in the world'. Bikers will argue forever whether this is just sales talk or whether it really is accurate. There are machines available with more electrifying performance or more exciting looks but on the road, in the average rider's hands, it is not easy to agree an obvious contender which stands clearly above a BMW. In 1982 the burden of the ultimate riding machine label is carried by a range of nine models. This chapter takes a detailed look at the latest offspring, the inheritance of the R32.

R100RS

Top of the range and, at first sight, looking vastly different from the R32, the RS was introduced in the autumn of 1976. Yet it was really only in its integrated fairing that this new model could be said to be different. Beneath the flying wedge there could still be found the traditional virtues of BMW design. It was a new generation vehicle, but it was clearly from the same mould.

Fairings had not generally been fitted by the factory until 1973 when the S, or bikini, type appeared on the R90S. This tiny handlebar fairing, designed by stylist Hans Muth, neatly integrated the instrument cluster of the Stroke models but offered the rider little real protection from the wind. Cosmetically, however, it looked smooth, setting off the air brush paint schemes which were now available alongside the traditional colours of black and white. As a design feature it was widely copied by the other manufacturers.

Previously, fairings had been huge, wrap-around aerodynamic shields fitted to the factory record-breakers or the cumbersome Glazier screens used on police models. These heavy

An R100RS on the limit (BMW).

fairings were attached to the forks and turned with the front wheel, but they were more of an identity symbol, a place to print POLIZEI, than an aid to high-speed riding. Tourers sometimes fitted proprietary screens to their BMWs, but they always tended to look extra and often upset handling in crosswinds. For the RS, Muth produced a new concept in fairing design which not only looked good and offered excellent rider protection against the elements, but it also significantly improved the bike's stability and handling at high speed. Wind tunnel testing was used to achieve the optimum airflow pattern around the bike and gain the most pleasing shape. Construction was of high quality glass-fibre and polycarbonate and the total fairing, although strong and rigid, only added 9.5 kg to the weight of the machine. It was futuristic in appearance and set a new style to the BMW look.

Experience with aerodynamic spoilers on racing cars had shown the ground-holding advantages which were possible and the same principles were applied to the RS fairing. Increased downthrust leads to better road holding and, with this fairing, the faster the bike was ridden the more stable it seemed to become. In this respect, the design was well ahead of the market where the fairings in use often led to uncontrollable weaving at really high speeds. Other bonuses included a reduction in drag helping with fuel consumption and an end to most of the wind buffeting which affects a motor cyclist. On a normal bike at 70 mph (112 km/h) this can cause considerable strain on arms and chest and forces the riding helmet uncomfortably into the neck.

The distinctive appearance of the RS fairing gave the bike a strong sporting image and this popular styling has helped to make the model a top seller. It has proved adaptable to a number of versions and kit forms make it available to pre-RS models. Tall riders complain that the airflow over the fairing results in buffeting to the helmet and some RS bikes have been fitted with an extension piece to the top of the screen. With the RS fairing it has proved difficult to fit the crash bars often used to protect the vulnerable-looking cylinder barrels of the flat twins. They can be fitted by cutting the fairing but some BMW mechanics consider that, in the event of a crash, the bars dig into the ground and cause extra damage. On 1981 models crash bars and a fairing make the already difficult task of changing the engine oil filter especially tiresome.

Riding the RS brings a special pleasure. It is a smooth blend of sports and touring capability packaged in an elegantly superior fashion. Press the electric start button and the 70 bhp motor spins into life and eagerly ticks over at just under 1,000 rpm. Open the throttle and the bike rocks slightly under the influence of torque reaction and impatience to hit the open road. Engage first gear, let out the clutch—now greatly lightened compared with earlier models—and the shaft drive instantly reacts lifting the rear of the bike up under acceleration and driving forward. It has taken BMW many years of continuous refinement to alter the characteristic 'clunk' of the first to second gear change, but drive shaft damping has made the latest models much quieter and easier in this respect. New riders will find that sudden downward gear changes on a BMW, as with all shaft drive systems, will cause the bike to twitch as the engine speed tries to match what is needed for the lower gear.

Speed is very deceptive on the RS, and all BMW models, because the power output is so relaxed. Newcomers to the bikes must check their speedometer constantly to keep within legal limits and to avoid rushing into corners. Acceleration is smooth and fast and it is possible to travel very quickly on

Wind tunnel tests for the R100RS integral cockpit (BMW).

Above left and right *Testing on the RS fairing was also done in real weather!* (BMW).

the RS and not signal the fact to the rest of the world by a screaming exhaust note. Braking is powerful and the three discs effectively cope with the machine's performance. The wet weather capability has benefited more from the recently introduced semi-metallic pads than the drilled plates of yesterday which probably offered more psychological comfort than real braking efficiency. Disc brakes were first used on BMWs in 1973 with the Stroke 6 series. At first, a single undrilled front disc brake was fitted to the R90 and the R75/6. The R90S came with twin front discs and it was claimed that drilling the plates helped to dissipate excess water and improved wet weather breaking. Riders found the single disc brake set up distorted steering under heavy braking and eventually the double disc arrangement became standard on the bigger models. Double front discs can be fitted as an extra to the R45 and R65 models. The RS now has disc brakes all round although some riders prefer a drum brake at the rear because it is claimed to give greater sensitivity. Perhaps significantly, the police still normally specify rear drums on their machines.

Heavy braking reveals another typical BMW idiosyncrasy which results from the practice of using long travel suspension units to ensure a comfortable ride. The 1981 RS features telescopic forks with double-acting hydraulic dampers and a huge 200 mm of suspension travel. At the rear, a swinging arm fork with three setting, progressive-rate shock absorbers gives 125 mm of suspension movement. The benefits are smooth travel over the bumpiest of surfaces and a substantial carrying capacity. The drawbacks are a pogo-like

Below *The aerodynamics of the RS integral cockpit.*

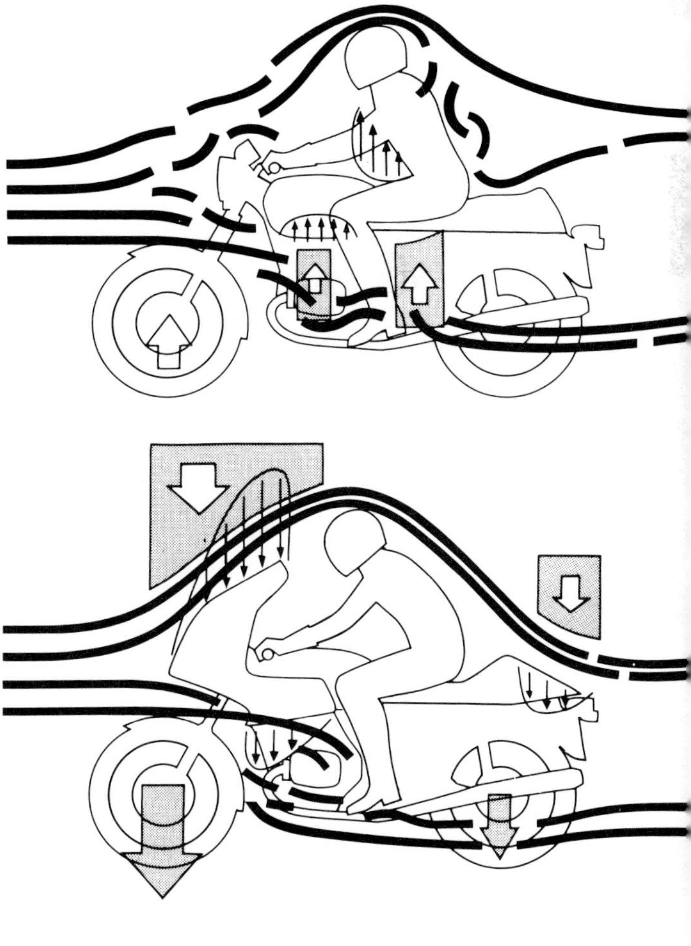

The R90S accelerating from 0 to 100 km/h in only 4.8 seconds (BMW).

bouncing as the front end dives under repeated heavy braking. This quality presumably gave rise to one German nickname for a BMW, *Die gummi Kuh*, the bouncing cow!

The RS is the latest in the line of BMW sports machines which date back to the breathed-on versions of the R32, the 1925 R37 and the 1927 R47. The 18 hp R47 still manages to win races in rallies for the old timers. Other notable sports versions were the R68, a 600 cc machine which appeared in 1952 as the first 100 mph production bike, and the 1973 R90S which was good for over 125 mph (200 km/h). Initially, the RS engine had the highest state of tune of all the BMW range making it clearly the sports model, but it now shares the same 70 bhp mill as the lighter R100CS and they have similar top speeds. By sports bike standards 200 km/h is not fast and bikes such as the Laverda Jota, the Honda 900 and even smaller Yamaha and Moto Guzzi models are all faster. However, BMW motor cycles have never stood for sheer, blood-curdling speed but rather high cruising rates and refinement. The RS allows the rider to use all its power in a relaxed and controlled way. It offers the everyday rider the simulation of racing with the reality of a safe and civilised town and country road bike.

R100RT

First introduced in 1978, this is the ultimate touring bike for the high mileage rider. It comes with a fully-equipped variation of the integral cockpit fairing especially designed for long-distance touring. This full-fairing has an adjustable windshield with integral air ducts and built-in lockable storage boxes. It offers very good weather protection, except noticeably to the hands, and is little affected by cross winds despite its size. As with the RS screen, the height of the rider can create problems which even the three-way adjustment cannot overcome. Tall riders may find the airstream over the screen buffeting their head and creating chilly draughts down their back; short riders may find themselves peering through the screen rather than over it. In such cases, although the plastic is optically quite good for vision, it remains open to doubt whether in law the bike should not be fitted with windscreen wipers like a car. A version of this fairing is fitted to many of the police BMW motor cycles.

The touring cockpit also houses the bike's instruments, which include a very accurate quartz clock. The idea of a clock on a motor cycle seems at first to be an unnecessary luxury, but it is surprising how useful it is and how often a rider refers to it for elapsed time calculations and checks on journey progress. The storage compartments are useful for maps and to hold the first aid kit which comes with BMW bikes; some owners even convert them to hold intercom sets. The air vents are of doubtful value in Europe where extra ventilation is seldom the requirement but they can be used to house retractable auxiliary headlamps which are available as an optional extra.

It was one of the early BMW claims that it had discovered an almost perfect riding position and certainly the sit-up stance on the RT is exceptionally comfortable. Although the high-rise handlebars and the big fairing are claimed by critics to make the RT cumbersome in slowly moving traffic, the bike steers very responsively at speed on winding roads. Handling on a motor cycle is also a function of weight distribution and suspension setting and the RT offers a novel solution to the latter. The latest RTs are fitted as standard with the Nivomat self-levelling suspension control. These automatic units are developed by BMW with the Boge company and can increase or decrease the effective suspension rate to suit the load or the going they sense. The extra weight of a pillion passenger and touring equipment normally taxes a motor cycle's suspension, but the Nivomats maintain ground clearance, which aids handling and helps to keep the headlight beam in the correct position for night time riding.

The gas/oil Nivomats are the latest in a line of suspension developments. In 1935 BMW led the world when maintenance-free telescopic forks with hydraulic shock absorbers were fitted to the R12, a 750 cc tourer. Three years later it was the turn of the rear of the bike and the R51 used telescopic plungers with helical compression springs. In the mid-'50s BMW persevered with the Earles type forks because of the steering rigidity which they provided, and recently the company has created a monolever rear suspension unit for its dual purpose R80 G/S machine.

The RT shares the same basic running gear as the RS with the fifth gear acting as an overdrive for economy touring. It can be ridden fast, being capable of 0-60 mph in under five seconds, or in

Above right *BMW touring style: the R100RT, the ultimate touring machine* (BMW).

Right *BMW self-adjusting Nivomat units, a recent BMW suspension development* (BMW).

The R61 with rear springing first introduced by BMW on its 1938 range (BMW).

silky silence with the intercom volume set at its lowest. On motorways it is steady and solid and in towns it has enough presence to be readily acknowledged by all the other vehicles, yet it is lively enough to exploit the holes in the traffic jams. Despite its bulk, the RT is something of a lightweight at 478 lb (217 kg) and could weigh in with most other makers' 650 cc machines. The RT has the near perfect balance of all BMWs and this makes dead handling, when parking, a relatively easy task. Owners not used to pushing four bags of cement around at a time are usually careful to avoid parking where there is a heavy camber or a loose surface. Some care needs to be taken in checking the centre stand on RTs at regular intervals as there have been a number of cases of these collapsing with embarrassing and costly results.

This long-legged tourer will transport its rider in any direction for trips of up to 500 miles (800 km) in perfect safety and comfort. That claim cannot be made in respect of the pillion passenger, however, and it is a matter for regret that the RT seats are less comfortable than those fitted to the earlier Stroke 7 models. Some BMW tourers dismayed by the RT seat have overcome their scruples at fitting non-standard parts and substituted pattern king and queen seats. An alternative is to change the RT seat, which has padding ridged up to contour into the tail fairing, and replace it by the straight Stroke 7 version.

R100CS

The classic sports version is distinguished by its nostalgic styling and the efforts which have been made to give it a good power to weight ratio. At 200 kg dry weight this makes the CS one of the lightest 1-litre motor cycles on the roads. The light, free-revving engine makes the CS very responsive and it will accelerate faster than any of the current BMW range. It is still not as fast, however, as its predecessor, the 100S. In town the CS is ever so slightly impatient trickling along at the legal limit and it requires only a twist of the throttle to send it hurtling down the road. As with all the big BMWs, under 3,000 rpm the wing mirrors are blurred because of pulsations set up in the offset cylinders of a flat twin. Beyond 3,000 rpm the blurring completely disappears.

The weight shedding on the CS has come mostly from the new lighter BMW engines and a less heavy braking system which includes a rear drum instead of a disc. Cylinder barrels are now all alloy with the bores coated in a wear-resistant silicon carbide lining called Galnikal. Apart from saving 3 kg in weight, this spray-on metal is claimed to increase engine life and it allows piston clearances to be tighter which means a quieter engine. Other

BMW R100CS Classic Sport (BMW).

weight savings have come from a lighter flywheel and clutch. This has also made a considerable change to the lightness of the controls and goes some way to meeting a criticism of BMWs that the heavy throttle and clutch are tiring on a long journey.

The original specification for the CS included wire-spoked wheels which were thought to be more in keeping with the 'classic' theme of the design than the cast type first adopted by BMW for the RS in 1976. Before BMW followed the fashion its light-alloy wheel rims with straight spokes for strength had been a feature of all its models since the R51/3 in 1951. Somewhat embarrassingly the wire wheels of the CS proved to be a failure and, with some 200 bikes built, BMW found it necessary to issue a recall notice. At speed it was possible for the spokes to flex and foul the disc brake caliper and collapse.

BMW's S models first appeared in 1960 when the tourers had their power uprated by increasing the compression ratio and fitting larger carburettors. The 26 bhp of the R50/2 became 35 bhp on the R50S, while the S version of the R69 found another 7 bhp. The R69S was the first production bike to come fitted with a hydraulic steering damper and it has since become recognised as one of the all time great BMWs.

Looking back to the 'Swinging '60s' these S models appeared bulky and heavy by comparison with similar makes of the time. The thoroughbred R100CS, despite the extra weight penalties of electric start and bigger batteries, is lithe and light and looks almost skinny against the present Japanese and Italian sports machines.

R100

This is the basic roadster tourer in the present BMW range. Described as a conservative model the R100 has been continuously developed and improved since 1976. It can claim to be a direct descendant of the R90/6 of 1973.

Utilitarian hardly describes this gentle giant, but it is the cheapest BMW 1-litre and it does come in basic trim. A low compression head and the lowest overall gearing, of the whole range gives the R100— reliability, easy maintenance, good handling, a considerate fuel consumption and genuine pulling power in all gears. For town or country the R100 is arguably the best all-rounder of the big BMWs.

Plainer than the sophisticated-looking RS and RT models and never likely to catch a CS on the road, the R100 can be fitted with special equipment and accessories. In the early days of the company BMW genuine extras ran to fundamentals such as headlights, sidecar mountings, oversize fuel tanks and even a rear

Above *The 1960 R50S, a USA version with high-rise bars* (BMW). **Below** *The R100 roadster* (BMW).

seat. Later, for export markets, modifications could include such things as high-rise bars, auxilary lighting, pannier frames and mudflaps. Today the list of accessories is endless and can easily transform an R100 into a very passable RS. Indeed, some British dealers have boosted their sales by dressing R100 machines in 'wolf's clothing' and thereby creating a cut-price RS.

R80 G/S

This all-purpose leisure bike is designed to give BMW performance and refinement both on and off the road. Conceived to recreate the freedom of 'anywhere travel', once the central object of biking, the 80 G/S makes exploration of the countryside an exciting possibility. The marvel of the machine is its incomparable performance on the road which is often a weak point with dual-purpose bikes. Indeed, it could sell purely as a road bike without pressing its off-road capability.

The R80 G/S was launched in September 1980 and, in several ways, is a radical departure for BMW. The suspension surprises with its unique monolever swinging arm and single spring shock-absorber rated for road and cross-country use. The parentage can be clearly traced from the works GS 80 machines of the late-'70s. Yet the long pedigree is there and BMW engineers have been building bikes able to tackle the rough with the smooth since the 1926 R37 which won the ISDT in the Isle of Man. Some BMW models such as the R4 and R35 were described as *Gelandesport Maschine*, although by modern standards they showed few special features for cross-country

The R80 G/S dual-purpose bike (BMW).

The R4, a successful off-road machine in the '30s (BMW).

work. By the mid-'50s trials styling showed on the R68 in the form of a high-level exhaust and off-road tyres. At first sight BMW styling seems too hefty for off-road use, but their dependability and massive low-down strength have frequently brought trials wins, especially in sidecar events. One of the most regular winners on the works special machines has been Sebastian Nachtmann, often captain of the German ISDT team.

By BMW standards the 80 G/S is electrifying to ride. On the road it is exceptionally sure-footed and it will respond in a very lively way to the throttle. It is a lightweight with a big heart and even on rough ground it is easy to handle and safe in any manoeuvre. The weight can, however, be a handicap in deep mud and the bike is more accurately described as an outstanding road machine with off-road potential. Contributing to its handling are specially developed tyres which give conventional grip and stability on the road at speeds up to 105 mph (170 km/h), yet will also work well on the rough. The monolever set up soaks up bumps very well and, as a bonus, permits the rear wheel to be changed in an instant. Unusual for an off-road machine the 80 G/S features a front disc brake. Quartz halogen lighting, full instrumentation and a big capacity fuel tank give the 80 G/S superior range and flexibility compared with the average enduro machines.

The R80 G/S has been designed to attract a new type of customer to BMW and it was planned with the German, French, Swiss and Italian markets very much in mind. In Britain the model has been slow to catch on. Unlike the continent, off-road riding here is not an established popular leisure time activity. The public's attitude to the dwindling countryside, strict conservation legislation and widespread property ownership restrictions, means that in Britain the opportunity to get out to the open spaces on a bike is rather limited.

As a mid-range tourer the 80 G/S can be tiring because of its wide, trials type handlebars and two-up riding is rather cramped. It seems likely, however, that the next obvious development step is to refine this dual-purpose machine by producing an all-roadster version. Such a model would be a useful addition to the range of BMW motor cycles and would satisfy those bikers who can appreciate performance but cannot afford the luxury and the expense of the bigger bikes.

R65

In the late '70s many of the world's motor cycle manufacturers introduced 650 cc models which gave big bike performance with the running costs of a middleweight. The 'superbikes' had become 'hyperbikes' and the market for expensive, petrol-guzzling heavyweights suddenly seemed over-crowded. The pendulum seemed to be swinging back to the high-speed but economical 650 twins of BSA, Enfield and Triumph. BMW recognised the trend and in 1978 produced the R65.

Compared with its parent the R75/7, the R65 is

leaner, lighter and smaller, but it is very nearly its equal in performance. Since its introduction the output of the R65 has been increased to 50 bhp and it possesses all the charisma of the bigger machines in a smaller and cheaper package. It handles safely and predictably at all speeds and it has light, easily managed controls. The cast wheels feature safety rims which will maintain riding stability even in the event of a complete blow-out. Lighting is of a high standard and at the rear is a special high-intensity brake light. Like all models since the Stroke 7 series the R65 has a lockable and recessed petrol filler cap which is cleverly leakproof in the event of the machine being dropped or crashed. One reversion to earlier models is the use of a single fuel petcock which requires angling the bike to get at the last drops of petrol in the tank.

A comparison between the 1981 R65 and the R60 of 20 years ago illustrates some of the ways in which BMW motor cycles have changed both in styling and function. The R60 was a tourer and for a while the number two in the range. It was considered ideal as a sidecar machine and it was widely used by the police in many countries. An optional extra for the R60 was a dualseat to replace the traditional BMW sprung saddle and separate pillion pad. The bike looked solid and heavy especially at the front end where Earles-type forks were fitted. Earles forks are considered aesthetically unacceptable today, but their great lateral strength, and the fact that they allow trail to be altered, made them very suitable for use with sidecars. It was also claimed that they reduced front end distortion at speed and gave some extra protection in the event of a head-on collision. As one young German rider claimed, 'Hit a car with an R60 and it would cut the car in half!' Like the R65

Right *The R60 teamed with a heavy touring chair* (BMW).

Below *The R65 is admired by BMW riders of tomorrow still learning their biking on mofas and mopeds* (BMW).

the R60 was fitted with 18-inch wheels which have been standard on BMW motor cycles since the mid-'30s. Before that enormous 26-inch tyres were the order of the day. In 1960 the R60/2 appeared with its 500 cc engine boosted to 30 bhp. A development model was the famous R69S, a fast sports version which won many track and record successes.

The R65 is a BMW compact clearly in the medium motor cycle class of the market. It is seen as a sports tourer and for the 1981 models the flat twin has been boosted to give extra bhp. A new frame geometry has been developed and, with the slim-line engine, the latest R65 is a nimble performer. For the LS variant the sports appeal has been accentuated by subtle styling devices rather than alterations to the flat twin engine. An optional extra on the standard R65 could be the RT type fairing to give full rider protection while touring. Traditionalists may see the pressed steel, mass-produced castings and colour-impregnated plastics of the R65 as a step backwards by BMW along the quality road compared with R60 days. In fact, strict adherence to over-engineering then nearly brought about the downfall of the company. Experience with the car side of the business clearly demonstrates to BMW that the most modern production methods are a commercial necessity. For the bikes the current approach is realistic without compromising the BMW image of quality to mass-market standards. The R65 may look leaner and hungrier than the R60 but the essential connection is still there.

R45

The stable companion to the R65 is a safe and dependable vehicle for the first time buyer and that purpose was part of its design brief. It may be a baby, but it is BMW through and through. In Germany learner rider legislation enables the 27 bhp version to be used for driving instruction. In fact, the machine is so reassuring and popular with learners that BMW produce a special riding schools version complete with conspicuous paint work and facilities for using intercoms.

In other world markets the R45 has been forced to compete with small capacity machines given an exciting sporting image to appeal to the younger riders. Mass marketing allows such bikes to be given frequent cosmetic changes to take advantage of the latest technical wizardry and to be in the fashion. By comparison the R45 is rather staid and uncompromising. For the experienced rider the R45, even in the 35 bhp version, seems rather gutless and it is the R65, using the same running gear, which appears to be the better way to acquire the BMW taste. Indeed, some dealers feel that BMW has never been a nursemaid to the motor cycle market and that it is the wrong machine for the job anyway. In Britain the height and weight of the R45 for inexperienced riders have been criticised, but its success in Germany only serves to illustrate how different world markets can be and the problems of getting a model mix right particularly, as with BMW, when the range is limited.

In the '60s and '70s the range followed the

The R45 engine, the current compact (BMW).

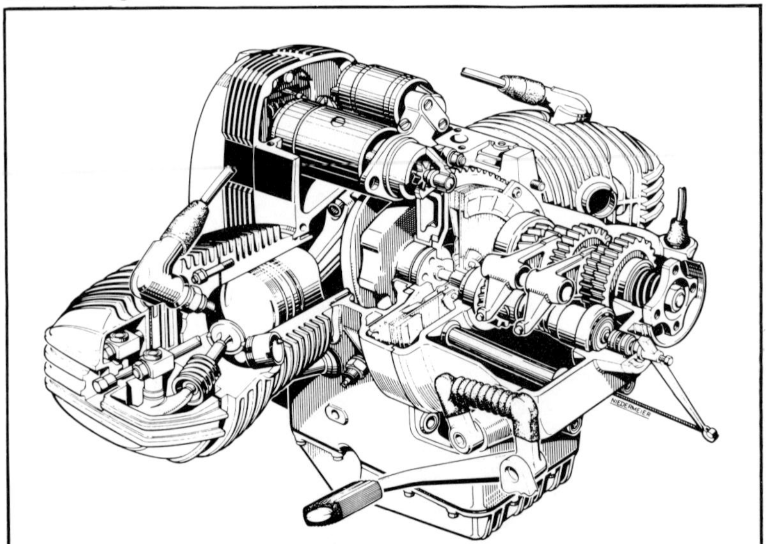

Inside a BMW single (BMW).

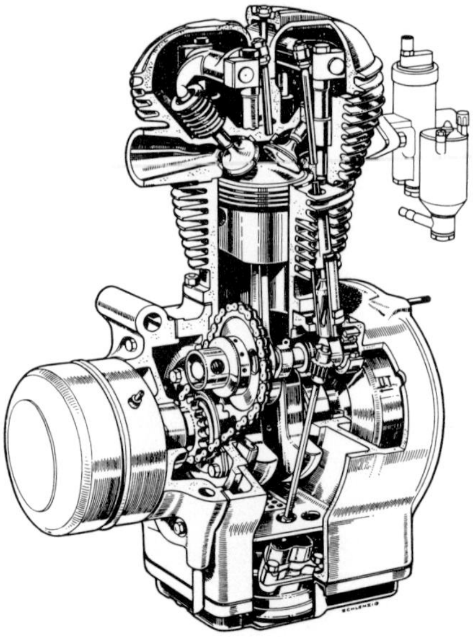

world trend to larger and more powerful bikes. The R45 concept originated from market research which indicated a need for a compact BMW which was less expensive, but did not sacrifice traditional qualities. BMW designers had been here before. Pre-war inflation and taxing policy created the utility machines and after 1945 a demoralised Europe need a bike with enough of the BMW stamp to distinguish it, but available to buyers who had set limits on the cost of motor cycling. In each case economy was achieved by settling for modest performance rather than reverting to a cheapened specification. The result in the elegant '80s is the R45, a bike which is almost as sophisticated as the bigger models, but does strain to keep its place. In less prosperous times baby BMWs had simpler, single-cylinder engines and basic accessories. The decision to make the R45 a twin is in keeping with a long held motor cycle convention, followed by BMW, that the 500 cc class is at the limit for single-cylinder machines. Just how the little ones used to slot into the range can be seen by comparing 1936 with 1981. 1936 was a vintage year for BMW motor cycles with a new world speed record (272 km/h) and high production output.

1936 range:

R2	—198 cc vertical single developing 8 bhp
R3	—305 cc vertical single developing 11 bhp
R4	—398 cc vertical single developing 14 bhp
R5	—494 cc flat twin developing 24 bhp
R12	—745 cc flat twin developing 18 bhp
R17	—734 cc flat twin developing 33 bhp

1981 range:

R45	—473 cc flat twin developing 27 or 35 bhp
R65	—650 cc flat twin developing 50 bhp
R80 G/S	—798 cc flat twin developing 50 bhp
R100	—980 cc flat twin developing 67 bhp
R100 CS	—980 cc flat twin developing 70 bhp
R100 RT	—980 cc flat twin developing 70 bhp
R100 RS	—980 cc flat twin developing 70 bhp

The first BMW single appeared as early as 1925 with the R39 and a small machine featured in the range up to 1938. After the Second World War the first machine the company was allowed to make was the R24, a development of pre-war singles. A prototype two-stroke flat twin with shaft drive, a genuine BMW miniature, never went into series production. The BMW single remained in production until 1967 when the 18 bhp R27 was discontinued. It was commonly used to pilot sidecars but, at the end of the '60s, such a heavyweight single was under severe competition from the many novelties emerging from the Japanese factories.

The company's 45-year history has clearly brought changes to the motor cycle range but faith to the original concept still shows through. Not yet for BMW riders the complexity of multi-valve cylinders or the untried technology of frequent model changes, ahead in fashion but subject to teething troubles, spares shortages and damaging to trade-in values. Instead, the BMW style is to build forward from what is known and respected. The BMW has kept pace with what modern biking needs, but it is still possible to see the roots.

The R25 single introduced in 1950 (BMW).

The ultimate working machine

Motor cycles are not just fun and leisure machines for those warm days of summer. The journey to work has often been a reason for bike purchase and the BMW's complete dependability has always made it very suitable for regular commuting. In fact, in Britain BMW owners still often use their bikes for the journey to work. Elsewhere the easy availability and convenience of the car, particularly in the winter, have relegated these bikes to leisure use only. Yet two-wheelers are perfectly suited for crowded city centres where their manoeuvreability and economy of convenience can be put to good use. Standstill time with a BMW motor cycle is minimal because of its long service life and mechanical reliability, its long range and its ability to guarantee extended periods of fatigue-free operation to the rider. These qualities have made BMW motor cycles an obvious choice for public authority work involving demanding patrol duties. Other users to appreciate this potential have included city courier services where the demand for fast, dependable delivery of documents, news items, drugs or computer tapes must be satisfied. In Washington DC a fleet of 60 Stroke 5 BMWs operate a year-round courier service which has helped to make that city a centre of BMW activity in the USA. In London, both the BBC and ITN use R65 fleets to speed film and information around the capital. In Germany the Allgemeiner Deutscher Automobil Club and in Britain the Automobile Association both use BMW motor cycles for their roadside assistance services to motorists. In Germany an R45 special comes fitted with CB radio and a fluorescent colour scheme for use as a driving school machine. At other times, BMWs have been used as light runabouts for haulage work and even for delivering the mail. Perhaps the most typical work has, however, been with the police and the military forces, and the rest of this chapter looks more closely at this application.

In the '30s the Germany Army, re-equipping under the impetus of the Third Reich, used models such as the R35, the R4, the R12 and later the R71 side-valve. The big machines were mostly fitted with an open sidecar and used for fast patrol work especially where the roads were steep or narrow and only suitable for light vehicles. Despite its

Below left *The BMW R45 driving school version* (BMW).

Below right *A German Army trials team on smart R5 500 cc machines gets some admiring glances from the young spectators* (AFN Ltd—the W.H. Aldington collection).

rigid springing the R4 was known to despatch riders as *Der Springer* (the jumper) and was widely used in off-road competitions by Army teams because of its excellent cross-country capabilities. Photographs of the times often feature the BMW-mounted German Army teams who were very successful in international trials events. One of the most famous team members was Sergeant-Major Georg 'Schorsch' Meier. Schorsch (a Bavarian nickname for George) was born in Mühldorf, 50 miles east of Munich, in 1910. He began racing seriously on an R4 in 1933 as part of the State police team. In 1937 he won the German Army championships as part of a military team known as the 'Cast Irons'. In the same year he began road racing at Hockenheim and this was to lead to the German and European Championships in 1938 and a string of grand prix victories in 1939 before the war interrupted his racing career. After the Second World War Meier gave German motor cycle sport, and BMW, continued heart by dominating road racing in Germany until 1953. In 1954 he helped to win a world speed record at Montlhéry on a 500 cc machine and he did not officially depart from racing until the Oldtimers Race at Salzburg in 1979. He now has extensive business interests in Munich and lives quietly in Switzerland. Apart from a brief spell with Auto Union just before the war Meier, arguably, did more to put the Max Friz concept on the world motor cycle map than anyone else.

Undoubtedly, the best known bike which BMW produced for the German war effort was the R75. It was developed in 1940 as the Wehrmacht's answer to the Jeep and was designed to be a complete cross-country vehicle. It had four road gears, four cross-country gears and two for reverse with a driven sidecar wheel. This gearing gave it a range from 3 km/h to 95 km/h and it could tow a tank! The R75 was capable of operation in any of the theatres of war, but it tended to be used almost exclusively in North Africa and on the Russian Front. In North Africa it was fitted with an extra large air filter to cope with the dusty air. For the Russian Front where temperatures could fall sometimes to -30 degrees C the crews could get some comfort from hand and foot warmers which used ducted hot gases from the exhaust system. The weight of an R75 with three crew and their weapons could be as much as a tonne and it certainly needed its reverse gears, its novel hydraulically operated brakes and the differential lock on the sidecar drive to keep it out of trouble.

There were few obstacles which the R75 could not

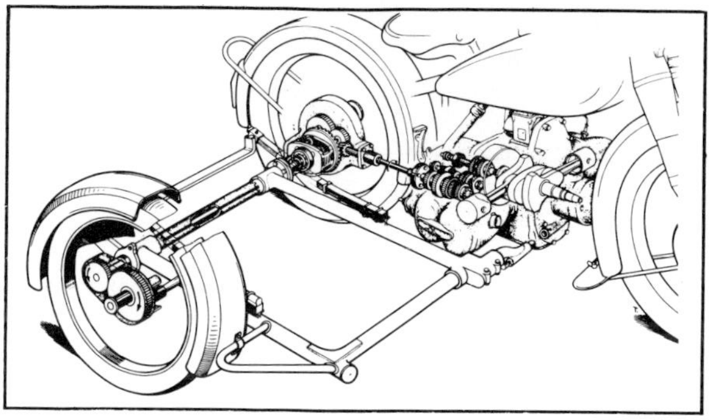

The working parts of the R75 (BMW).

tackle and its high mounted air filter even allowed it to traverse quite deep water. The outfit did, however, require a good deal of skill to use and it proved less adaptable and flexible than the easy-drive, go-anywhere Jeep. The R75 was built in BMW's Eisenach factory and between 1941 and 1944 some 16,500 were put into use. The original development was supervised by Dipl Ing Alex von Falkenhausen who had joined the company in 1934. Some credit must also go to Zündapp designers who created the differential gear drive to the two rear wheels. Zündapp produced a similar vehicle to the R75 as part of their war efforts, which was designated the KS 750 and which is now nicknamed the 'green elephant'. In fact, the idea of a flat twin with a driven sidecar was not completely new and versions had been developed before the war by the Belgian FN company and Gnome-Rhone in France. The Gnome-Rhone motor cycles were derivatives of the ABC flat twins which had been built in France under licence since 1920. As many of these combinations fell into the hands of the Germans in the early stages of the war in Europe it seems likely that their best features influenced the design of the R75.

After 1955 the Bundeswehr was formed as part of the NATO Alliance and for a while BMW again provided military bikes in the form of modified R26 and R27 250 cc models. At the time of writing the Hercules company provides all the motor cycle needs of the Federal Defence Force.

The BMW concept has also proved to be an ideal one for police duties. Before the end of the '20s the German police were BMW-mounted and in the 1930s German traffic police patrols used sporty R51 machines. In the '50s the typical police bike in Germany was an R50 equipped with heavy polizei fairing, blue light and pillion-mounted radio. Some were white and known familiarly as the *Weiß mice.* By the time the Stroke series bikes were introduced international policing by BMW motor cycle had become a reality. Currently, the public authorities in 83 countries from Abu Dhabi to Zambia rely on BMWs for patrol and escort work. The company offers a total of ten different models for public authority use and a long list of factory-fitted accessories are available for specific requirements. Some of these extras have proved acceptable to the ordinary BMW owner and are now more widely available. One example is the extra-deep front mudguard which gives better protection against road mud than the standard fitting on BMW bikes. Some RT machines are now seen with a civilian version of the retractable identification lights which can be fitted in the air ducts of the police fairings. The full list of options available is very comprehensive and includes special engine modifications, running gear accessories and many special electrical possibilities.

Top *German traffic police on parade with their R51 BMWs* (BMW).

Above La Gendarmerie Nationale *in France are equipped with BMWs. These R50s have now been replaced by R80 TIC* (E.C.P. Armées).

Left *Retractable identification lights, one of the factory options for public authority BMWs* (BMW).

Special equipment which can be factory-fitted by BMW to their public authority motor cycles

Engine options: Reduced compression ratio (for countries where premium fuel has a low octane rating), a kick starter, a heel and sole foot shift, oil cooler and full suppression for interference-free communications.

Running gear options: The touring integral cockpit, Nivomat self-levelling units, a heavy duty suspension for rough riding terrain, cast or spoke wheels, dual disc brakes on the smaller models, a steering damper where road conditions are particularly poor.

Electrical options: Alternating tone horns, siren, identification lights in red or blue, a 360 degree accident light, hazard warning flashers, electrical socket.

Other options: High-rise handlebars, twist grip friction control adjuster so that traffic signals can be given without a sudden loss of speed, a tank with extra stowage space, a single seat, touring mudguard, rear mudflap, cylinder and rear protection bars, leather and plastic panniers.

Where BMWs are used for public authority purposes

Abu Dhabi; Afghanistan; Algeria; Andorra; Angola; Argentina; Austria; Belgium; Benin; Brazil; Burma; Cameroon; Central Africa; Chile; Colombia; Comores; Congo-Brazzaville; Curaçao; Denmark; Djibouti; Dominican Rep; Ecuador; Egypt; Ethiopia; Finland; France; Gabon; Ghana; Greece; Great Britain; Guinea-Bissau; Guinea-Conakry; Hungary; Iran; Israel; Italy; Ivory Coast; Jordan; Korea, North; Korea, South; Kuwait; Liberia; Libya; Luxembourg; Madagascar; Mali; Mauretania; Morocco; Netherlands; Niger; Nigeria; Norway; Oman; Paraguay; Peru; Philippines; Portugal; Qatar; Rumania; Senegal; Sierra Leone; Somalia; South Africa; Spain; Sudan; Surinam; Sweden; Switzerland; Taiwan; Tchad; Togo; Tunisia; Turkey; Upper Volta; Uruguay; USSR; Venezuela; West Germany; Yemen; Yugoslavia; Zaire; Zambia.

The smart appearance of BMWs makes them very suitable for official escort duties. In a number of countries a special squad of BMW motor cycles is used for royal or presidential ceremonial.

One of the most significant successes in winning contracts to supply public authorities with motor cycles has come in its almost complete domination of the British police bike market. Until the '70s British police forces invariably used Triumph Saint or Norton Commando machines for traffic patrol work. Neither model was considered ideal for the job, but it was clearly presumed that British police would ride British bikes. The chief problem was vibration, the inherent design weakness of a vertical twin layout. The bikes literally shook their special equipment to pieces and spent as much time off the road as on it. Rider fatigue was undesirably high and this led to a loss of police efficiency. Matters had been made considerably worse at this time because the British motor cycle industry was in a state of near collapse following the Japanese domination of the market. Wracked by closures and takeovers the Triumph and Norton spares service was simply too unreliable for police needs.

When David Willcox was appointed Force Transport Officer to the Thames Valley Police in 1972 he found that half his fleet of Nortons and Triumphs were off the road awaiting spare parts. Even the much praised Norton suspension quickly shook radios apart and there were continual problems with crankshafts, pistons and chains. It was even proving difficult to maintain suitable cover for the duty rosters. Encouraged by his Chief Constable, David Willcox wrote to all the major motor cycle manufacturers and asked for a product evaluation. Surprisingly, there was little interest from the Japanese and it was Moto Guzzi and BMW which answered the call. Following evaluation tests the BMW bike was preferred by all the police riders who liked its vibration-free performance and reported no significant fatigue after hours in the saddle on a typical duty shift.

By October 1972 NPP 728L and NPP 729L, two standard R75/6s were operating out of the Aylesbury and Slough police stations. The bikes were painted white and they had high-rise handlebars. The Thames Valley police added an Avon fairing, a blue light, two-tone horns, panniers and a radio at the rear. At first the handset was fitted on the tank top but later this was considered a potential danger in the event of an accident and it was moved. They were the first two BMWs to be put into service by a British police force. The repercussions were immediate and dramatic. Questions were raised in Parliament, the Press fuelled public criticisms

Left *The controversial advertisement* (Smee's Advertising Ltd).

Below *The handing over presentation of the 1,000th police BMW to the Hampshire Force in 1979. In the foreground is NPP 728L, the first BMW motor cycle used by the British police and registered on November 16 1972* (Thames Valley Police).

Below right *BMW and the law* (BMW).

with headlines about the British police buying foreign and the Chief Constable, David Holdsworth, even received anonymous threatening letters. Trade unions debated the consequences for their members in the dying Midlands motor cycle industry and the rest of the police forces looked on with coy interest.

The police riders enjoyed using such a quality machine and approved of the public interest in their bikes. Heads were turned as they passed by and, because the BMWs were found less tiring to use, the police found themselves better humoured in their dealings with the public. The bikes were manoeuvrable, they handled well in the chase and, with their low-slung pots well out in the airstream, they proved ideal for slow speed escort duty for abnormal loads.

The police mechanics were satisfied because the BMWs proved to be completely reliable and predictable. Service intervals could be properly rostered and, with wear virtually a known factor, it was found unnecessary to carry large stocks of spares other than immediate consumables such a as plugs, lamps, filters and brake pads. Eventually it was to prove possible to service 86 BMWs with the same number of mechanics as was originally required to keep 60 Triumphs and Nortons on the road.

The police authority was pleased to approve further purchase of BMWs, despite their relatively high price, because they so easily met operational needs and had low running costs. At this time the official disposal mileage of a Triumph Saint was 40,000 miles (64,000 km) although the Thames Valley police found that they were lucky to get 25,000 miles (40,000 km) of actual use. The anticipated mileage for the first BMWs was set at 80,000 (130,000 km) and, in fact, both machines did over 100,000 miles (160,999 km) before being sold in 1980. In 1974 the Thames Valley police bought 15 BMWs and by 1978 had gone over completely to the brand.

The conversion of the rest of the British police forces to BMW machines was one of the sales triumphs of the British concessionaires at Chiswick. The police business was seen as a priority marketing venture and not something which should be left to the initiative of local dealers. Understandably this action was not greeted with universal approval by the trade! Eventually BMW Concessionaires GB appointed Neale Shilton to run the public authorities business. He had already established a reputation amongst the police forces selling Triumph Saints and Norton Interpols. With his BMW offer he was to prove almost irresistible and in a four-year period most of the British police traffic patrol work was switched to the Bavarian twins. In 1975 four UK police forces had 50 R80/7 patrol bikes on duty but by 1980 48 of the public authorities out of 55 had purchased 2,000 machines between them.

This creation of a police market for BMW motor cycles in Britain did not proceed entirely smoothly. The notorious BMW advertisment of 1972 'It Takes One to Catch One' probably set

Above *An R75/6 in use by the Greek police on Corfu in 1981* (Author).

Left *Neale Shilton of BMW* (GB).

Above right *Munich police prepare to escort a group of Japanese dealers on the 1981 RS Rideaway* (BMW).

back the plans of the Thames Valley police to go BMW by a year, according to David Willcox. This advertisment was brilliantly conceived by Smee's Advertising Ltd, a well-established London advertising agency with interests in the motor trade, who were doing PR work for BMW at the time. The advert used real Thames Valley policemen and their vehicles and created a minor sensation when it appeared in the national Press. Widely admired as an advertising scoop it proved counter-productive in the delicate negotiations which were then being carried out to persuade the public authorities to buy foreign. On another occasion, a senior BMW manager was actually booked for speeding and impersonating a police officer while trying to deliver a police specification bike to one of the Forces for evaluation!

Potentially the most serious problem concerned the Sussex Constabulary in 1976. Sussex police riders had two serious crashes while evaluating

their BMWs and concluded that they were inherently unsuitable for police work because of a tendency to high-speed weaving. The timing was critical because following the decision of the City of London police to buy BMWs in 1975 there were several key orders in the balance. BMW Concessionaires quickly responded by organising a special test day for the police with the bikes set up in factory-approved style. The results were conclusive for the rest of Britain, although not for Sussex who remain one of the few forces not to ride BMWs. Staunch allies through these difficulties were the Thames Valley police who gave demonstrations and reported on the BMWs' behaviour under service conditions.

Naturally police riders soon put big mileages on a bike. The Thames Valley police average about 2,000 miles (3,200 km) a month on their machines. This kind of all weather work soon sorts out a bike's strengths and weaknesses and the BMWs have stood up remarkably well to this treatment. The bikes do, of course, benefit from regular servicing at 3,500-mile (5,600 km) intervals and they are constantly in the hands of professionals. It is part of a patrol rider's responsibility to check and wash the bike daily. Experience has shown that those vulnerable pots have never been grounded, no shaft drive system has ever given trouble and official disposal mileages have easily been exceeded. Weaknesses have been found in rusting exhausts, the original batteries not standing up to the demands of police work and a problem which was found to be due to over-zealous cleaning of the rear hub assembly. From a big mileage point of view the Thames Valley police also find that transistorised ignition has considerable advantages and that Metzeler tyres are superior to Michelin covers. Significantly, the police recommend that BMW tyres are changed as soon as the tread pattern drops below 3 mm.

5

The ultimate touring machine

User surveys show repeatedly that BMW owners tend to ride considerably more than the national average annual motor cycle mileage. This is because owners use their bikes for touring at the weekends and for their annual holidays. One of the most frequently stated reasons for buying a BMW rather than any other make is its special suitability for touring.

Motor cycling has always attracted a dedicated group who ride purely for the pleasure it gives. Biking for them might almost be described as an addiction. Not for them the restricted view and the passive contact with the countryside which the vinyl-padded and carpeted motor car can offer. They prefer to feel the world as it rushes by them rather than isolate themselves in an air-conditioned container. Their pleasure comes from breathing real air which is alive with smells informing the senses that there are pinewoods nearby or the passing town has a brewery. Their thrill is the steady beat of the engine eating up a long journey, passing other vehicles and always so close, so dangerous and yet so controlled. At the journey's end the machine is stopped, the adrenalin flow slows and the full pleasure of the ride can be appreciated as the tension eases. Motor cycling retains the excitement of travel, something which gets lost in the motor car. Motorists are often more occupied by the in-car entertainment than the passing scene. Bikers are much more concerned with the immediate and what is happening around them. Indeed, they have to be because a momentary lack of concentration is all it needs for disaster to arrive. It involves closely reading the road down to the detail of minor bumps, patches of damp leaves, the pattern of manhole covers and even changing temperature and humidity. It also means being aware of fatigue and the need for appropriate rest periods. At journey's end a biker has travelled not in a time machine or space transporter but in a corridor of mental alertness. It will have involved catching some of the qualities of the landscape rather than passing through as an uninvolved spectator.

It takes a motor cycle as good as the BMW to make such adventures come to fruition. A BMW is such a good tourer because it offers a happy compromise between creature comforts and the sometimes harsh reality of biking. The genuine elements of riding a motor cycle are there but in a sophisticated package which eliminates much of the hassle. Touring is patently not about sitting at the roadside changing plugs or adjusting a slack and oily chain. Nor is it constantly worrying about where the next petrol station is, or being forced to speed along the motorways because two-up and with luggage the bike will not handle on minor roads where the scenery is. The full pleasure of

Touring BMW style with the concrete flashing beneath the feet (BMW).

Heavily laden BMWs, many of them comprehensively equipped for long-distance touring, at the International BMW Rally, Saxmundham, Suffolk, July 25-26 1981 (Author).

touring only comes when a rider knows that the bike will go anywhere, anytime with total reliability and comfort.

All the BMWs have touring ability although the extra performance of the RS and the RT identifies them as the Grand Tourers. The BMW characteristics which appeal to the tourer have been well-proved over the years. The big, flat twin motor has plenty of tractable power and will happily cruise all day at the legal limits regardless of loading. The bikes handle well on the motorway, in town and, significantly, along the back country lanes. Long, soft suspension travel makes the ride comfortable and 500 miles (800 km) on a loaded RT are possible with little rider or passenger fatigue. The economical engines, coupled with large-capacity fuel tanks, mean that over 200 miles (300 km) are possible between garage stops. BMW has never expected the tourer to interrupt a journey to carry out routine adjustments at the roadside and peace of mind over matters mechanical allows full attention to be given to the pleasures of the ride. The very comprehensive tool kit provided on all BMWs is a sensible accessory when touring. No mechanical equipment can be totally foolproof and after 2-3,000 km any motor cycle will require a checkover to keep it in optimum running condition. The simple layout of the BMW engine and drive system means that such basic checks are easy to do and quickly completed. The tradition of totally enclosing the engine takes out some of the problems of cleaning up touring grime. Even a crisis such as a puncture, which will tend to happen at a busy road junction or when the weather is at its worst, is easy to handle with quick release half shafts rather than messy drive chains.

It is remarkable how much in the way of clothes and equipment a couple can use when touring and a BMW motor cycle has a very superior carrying capacity. There is plenty of space on an RT in its pannier cases, tank bag, tail fairing and cockpit boxes. A lot of heavy gear could be carried while still remaining well within the permissible gross weight of 970 lb (440 kg). Moreover, BMW's design means that this load-bearing equipment is strong and complements the machine. BMW panniers, for example, are designed for high speed touring at up to 80 mph (130 km/h) and will not adversely affect the bike's handling. The panniers can be colour-matched to the bike and quick release catches instantly convert them into smart touring luggage. Other official touring refinements include heated handlebar grips for all-weather rides, auxiliary driving lights, hazard warning flashers and additional tools and spares kits as security for the prudent. Add the advantages of the integral fairing designed to extend performance and provide a safe, relaxed riding position and the BMW touring specification is certainly difficult to better.

Regular tourers will often go beyond the official extras and customise their machine with modifications found to be useful while on the road. In the USA, where long-distance touring is a way of life, such accessories are big business. BMW tourers not only fit big capacity Heinrich tanks but many also add colour matched auxiliary tanks around the side panels. A popular conversion to dual plugs on each cylinder is said to increase fuel economy and give better all round performance. Some tourers fit throttle friction screws so that the right hand can be relaxed on long open roads without losing speed. The integral fairings offer plenty of scope for modifications from fitting flip-out type headlights to wiring in CB radio, on road Hi-Fi or installed driver/pillion intercom sets. Other fairing accessories include wind deflectors and hand protectors for the S type. Long hours in the saddle may encourage the fitting of twin bucket seats or a back rest for the pillion rider. Extra instrumentation can include

Above *Well-kitted up for the worst of winter, an R17 combo with elegantly slim Steib chair* (AFN Ltd—the W.H. Aldington collection).

Below *A dusty pair of shaft-driven tourers arrive at Arilles, Corfu, after a long run from Wiesbaden* (Author).

the luxury of an oil temperature gauge dipstick to give a direct reading of the engine oil. An extra which many owners feel should be standard on a motor cycle of this quality are stainless steel silencers.

The question of how far to go with accessories is a common talking point wherever tourers meet. Some purists hold that only genuine BMW-approved extras should adorn their bikes. Others will allow anything that is sensible and adds to the safety or efficiency of the machine as a tourer. A typical issue might be whether it is right to stick plastic protection tape over paintwork or plating to save wear or to simply let the BMW beauty fade naturally.

Such a question can become an issue because a commitment to touring brings an owner closer to the machine. Getting anywhere involves a two-way relationship that requires a sense of empathy. The bike's personality becomes known and understood and leads some owners to give their BMWs names. Instinctively the rider comes to know how much choke is required to start, the best pressure for the tyres, when to refill the tank, how best to load luggage and retain good handling and the most comfortable speeds to adopt in order to bring distance, physical stress, engine noise and suspension movement all in to harmony. Touring is not just a question of long distance, but of the perfect ride. This comes from being in the right location, having the bike set up well and meeting the right sort of travelling companions.

Tourers naturally vary in the demands which they make on their machines and the history of

BMW motor cycles is littered with epic journeys across continents or gruelling tests of achievement such as journalist Dave Minton's ride on a Stroke 7 to the North Cape in the winter of 1978. This test of man and machine involved a three-week trip in temperatures down to -30 degrees C along the Arctic Highway to Kirkeness. More recently, Danish born superbiker Hans Tholstrup completed an 18-day marathon ride on an R80 G/S which took him 12,500 miles (22,000 km) from London across Europe and the Middle East to India, by sea to Perth and then across Australia to Sydney.

For the more typical BMW tourer the season normally runs from spring to autumn and will include some week-end runs, longer trips to rallies or road racing and probably a period of extended touring during the annual holiday. In Europe BMWs can be seen gently ticking in the heat of the Mediterranean coast having brought their owners south for the sun. Europe is, of course, well served by BMW official agents and the tourer need never be far from friends. The guide to BMW dealers gives details of BMW service in 18 countries and even includes Moscow Service Station No 7 (situated on 2, Selskochosjajstwennij) which covers the whole of the Soviet Union! In the USA Beemers, as they are often called, are ridden or trailered to Daytona in the spring and the West Coast at other times. The laden BMW tourer American-style can reach new heights with its touring gizmos. Enhancements include strengthened ride-off stands, cushion handgrips to reduce vibration, daylight running lights with a flicker effect, tail-lights which work in unison with the turn signals, customised paint jobs and even trailers to carry Koolpacs, tents and other essential touring items. They stand in direct contrast to some of the tourers who occasionally emerge from behind the Iron Curtain proudly running wartime vintage BMWs on original or home-produced parts. Typical might be Czech tourer, Václav Hamsik who used his R61 combination in 1979 to make a 2,200-mile (3,500 km) tour from his home in Gottwaldov to Sweden. Two friends who often go with him ride an R75 *Gespannmaschine* and a 1938 R12. The staying power of the R75 and its riders is also illustrated by British rider Fred Horton who regularly tours Europe at the age of 75.

In Australia touring is often on a grand scale with BMW owners thinking little of riding across the world to the 'old country'. In their outback Australian tourers report exciting clashes with giant road trains on the single track bitumen roads

Václav Hamsik and his family pose with their R61 touring combo. The outfit was fitted with Norton handlebars and front mudguard and a Jawa seat for this trip, although the original parts have been saved (Václav Hamsik).

of Northern Territory. Roads can become soft sand tracks with no petrol or water for 200 miles (320 km) but a BMW invariably gets there even if it does mean second or third gear for the heavy machine. However, one of the longest BMW trips must be the 95,000-mile (152,000 km) ride by Daniel Liske on an R60 from Alaska to the southern tip of South America. He later took a shorter spin from northern Sweden to South Africa covering a mere 40,000 miles (64,000 km). These journeys compare with Ted Simon's world epic on a Triumph which took four years (1973-77) and covered 54 countries and 63,000 miles (100,000 km).

Some idea of how the concept of touring has changed in 40 years can be judged by comparing the ohv R66 with a modern counterpart, the R65S. The R66 was derived from the R6, one of BMW's last plonking side-valvers. It delivered 30 bhp and typically was expected to be paired with a chair. At the 1938 Olympia Show in London all the BMW range were dressed with a sidecar. Unlike today, BMW frames were then constructed with sidecar fixing lugs to take the graceful Steib chairs. The powerful R66 had plunger rear springing and used the running gear of the R51. For touring it could be fitted with a sprung pillion saddle which floated in sympathy with the rider's seat. A tool box was set in the top of the fuel tank and the speedometer, compared with earlier models, had been moved from the tank to be inset

Top *BMW R66, 600 cc sidecar sports model* (BMW).

Above *Restorer's art, an R27 on show at the International BMW Rally in 1981* (Author).

Below *An R27, slightly modified, but still in daily use on the rough roads of north-west Corfu* (Author).

in the headlamp nacelle. It still retained, however the additional hand lever introduced with the R5 to help the rider select neutral and as a back-up to the new foot-operated gear change. The deep, extended front mudguard, alas no longer acceptable to the stylists, kept road dirt from the engine and the rider. The riders then toured in heavy, black, oilskin storm-coats, gauntlets, rubber boots and flat cap. The alternative BMW riding gear was the waxed cotton suit which offered excellent weather protection but had a distinctive smell of the outdoors and was something of a liability off the bike. Now the BMW tourer can enjoy clothing which is not only functional but is elegantly styled to complement his bike.

It does not need 40 years of history to create this contrast of images and tourers often typify the 'two worlds' theme of the BMW story. On one side is the genuine BMW enthusiast, probably owning an R60 and certainly nothing made after 1969 when, many consider, BMW stopped building motor cycles. De rigueur dress is the black Barbour roadsuit with, reluctantly and somewhat irrelevantly, an open-face helmet. Ownership means frequent cleaning and tuning, membership of the BMW club and regular touring holidays. Occasionally the love affair with BMW involves a long, painstaking and accurate renovation of an old model to concours elegance. This will be proudly displayed at rallies and become the subject of numerous treasured photographs in the albums of fellow enthusiasts. New technology and the bolt-on accessories are often seen as a threat to the true values of motor cycling.

At the other extreme is the owner who is simply enthusiastic about BMW motor cycles. The bike is bought on reputation and is seen more as a means of transport than an object of worship. It is allowed to get dirty and is expected to perform in all weathers and conditions. The owner, not being especially interested in the mechanics, leaves servicing to the dealer and only has it done at approved intervals. Because the bike is not nursed parts fail at normal mileages and this owner cannot match the extraordinary claims of some enthusiasts to ever-lasting tyre covers or anorexic fuel consumptions. Improvements are welcomed for making biking easier and more comfortable and price is rarely questioned because it is accepted that, as a BMW represents the best, they will cost more. It is, perhaps, part of the marque's success that it can continue to satisfy both worlds. The power of unlimited freedom is what BMW motor cycling is about and it hardly matters whether that pleasure comes from a colour-matched RT bowling along some Riviera autoroute or Václav Hamsik's patched, black R61 swinging north on to the E15 at Dresden just 260 km east of its birthplace in the old Eisenach factory.

One way for tourers to keep in touch is through the activities of the owners clubs throughout the world. These clubs encourage motor cycling the BMW way and arrange local riding events and tours to rallies in other countries. The BMW club was founded in 1952 and was first called by the grand title the BMW Society of Great Britain. Today the club in Britain is administered nationally but is divided into 11 regional sections covering the North, the North-East, the Midlands, the West, Ireland, the South-West, Oxford, the South-East, London and East Anglia to meet the needs of local groups of owners. There are affiliated clubs operating in Australia, Belgium, Canada, France, Italy, Poland, South Africa, the USA, West Germany and Zimbabwe. Members communicate through club activities and the correspondence pages of the club journals. BMW itself no longer circulates a house magazine, although before the Second World War it issued regular editions of the *Blatter*. In the '70s BMW Concessionaires (GB) had a house journal called *Torque* and there is a plan by BMW(GB) to launch one with the title *Image*.

The club journals contain articles of general interest to BMW owners such as descriptions of tours or modifications which can be made to the bikes to improve performance. Members gain useful and interesting insights into the technical and historical side of BMW ownership and the letters pages allow complacency to be shattered by angry letters of frustration. From time to time outraged owners will write blaming BMW or the importers for permitting standards to decline. The basis of complaint is usually that their new machine, hardly run-in, now needs a new gearbox, has a duff ignition, an irritating vibration at 4,250 rpm and the paintwork is peeling. More practically useful are the letters giving tips on how to maintain peak performance and the advertisement pages for specialist accessories purporting to improve the Ultimate! For the new owner this can sometimes rank with the mystique which surrounds hobbies such as HiFi and photography. Does the average ear really discriminate between wow and flutter of 0.03 per cent and 0.04 per cent WRMS or will this 3X converter really make all the difference to your snapshots? The professed enthusiast seems to think so and hence the continuous debate. One advertisment will claim that the simple and well-tried points system on the Stroke 7 bikes can be changed to electronic ignition to give better starting and fuel economy. How much better can be arguable when it is considered what a variety of factors other than timing affects them both. Similarly there are claims that the ride of an RT can be significantly improved by fitting special air suspension units or its performance boosted by purchasing a 'sport pak'. It all adds up to the sense of belonging to a very exclusive group and certainly keeps the topic of conversation lively at club meetings.

Top *A finely restored 1938 R12 belonging to Josef Sovjak of Gottwaldov, Czechoslovakia* (Václav Hamsik).

Above *The 1954 R68, the '100 mph machine'* (BMW).

Other bonuses from BMW club membership include schemes such as a specialist tool hire service and various discounts negotiated with parts and accessories suppliers. Over the question of discounts, manufacturers, importing companies and dealers rarely see the issue from the same perspective as owners clubs. For the former idealism must be partly tempered by the need to make profits and expectations of preferred treatment by the club membership are sometimes seen as hopelessly unreasonable. In extreme cases club members are seen as fanatics dedicated to a dream of gleaming, faultless bikes and expecting, as of right, priority treatment in the event of any problems. For their part club members are so passionate about their machines that they feel ownership and support for the marque entitles them to some privilege. In particular, BMW owners become vocal at any suggestion of down-grading the image of the ultimate riding machine. This watching brief extends not only to the maintenance of the technical standard but the credibility of the service and sales strategies of the importers.

If you ask a BMW owner to name his favourite model, you will know the man. A new member will probably select the R65LS, the latest in the current range and incorporating typical BMW values of high technology and a sporting appearance. The middle-aged poseur will go for the glamour of the RS while a tourer might settle for the luxury conveniences of the RT. The generation gap begins to show with those who claim that it is necessary to go back before the Stroke series to find the real BMW motor cycles. How many BMW enthusiasts, for example, would go along with Charles Lock, one of the founder members of the BMW club, and now living in Australia, who rates the 1954 R68 as the finest BMW ever? Jock West has ridden many BMW bikes in his time, on the race track, in trials and on the road and he has particularly fond memories of the virtues of the R71. The favourite of Alf Cook, spannerman to the record-breaking MLG race team in the early '60s, was an R51/3 which was so finely set up that he could start it by hand! Frank Cox of Markhouse Motor Cycles and, probably, one of the most knowledgeable BMW enthusiasts in Britain, is one of many who feel that the R69S was the best model ever produced. The author found little to criticise in a faithful R75/7 although recent test rides on the R80 G/S and the R65LS have proved exciting and memorable. There can, of course, be no final answer as personal perception is impossible to evaluate. Today's model line up is not just a question of tradition and engineering compromises—it is complicated by marketing and styling considerations, by cost-effective production limitations, by export

John Ebbrell of Motor Cycle Weekly *tries the ex-Afrika Korps R75 restored, complete with Wehrmacht ammunition boxes and divisonal sign, by Belgian brothers, Hubert and Franz Vervoort—wearing the woolly hats. Typical of the machines attracted to the Elephant Rally in 1969* (Motor Cycle Weekly).

The hardy rallyists of the Elefantentreffen—now held at the Salzburgring (Motor Cycle Weekly).

requirements and the general economic situation. The uniqueness of BMW is that it continues to thrive as a world force in motor cycle manufacture despite mass production, mass marketing and the accountants.

Talk of the classic bikes is often the tent-side conversation at rallies where the full variety of touring can be experienced. Riders will cross continents to attend a bike rally which may be little more than a gathering of enthusiasts in a muddy field. Lately, some rallies have gone up-market with discos, field sports and organised entertainments, but the traditional rallyist remains content with a parking space, a spot to pitch a tent, freedom to gaze at the other bikes and plenty of opportunity to talk shop. The BMW clubs organise camping weekends, navigation tests, treasure hunts and mystery tours for members. Once a year national rallies in each country attract long-distance tourers from the international membership. The 1981 BMW Owners Club of America rally, for example, was held at Loretta Lynn's Dude Ranch near Hurricane Mills, Tennesee. It attracted over 6,000 participants who rode in on 3,400 BMWs. The youngest rider was a girl of 15 years on an R75/5 and 17 bikes and their riders were brought over from Britain and France to take part.

A unique rally for BMW motor bikes is the Elephant *(Der Elefantentreffen)*, West Germany's biggest, oldest and best known rally. This mid-winter event was started in 1956 when Ernst Leverkus and friends with 30 bikes gathered at the Solitude race track near Stuttgart. The meeting place later changed to the Nürburgring in the Eifel Mountains and by 1976 was attracting as many as 15,000 bikes. The venue now is Austria's famous Salzburgring and the event takes place in the first week of February when sub-zero temperatures and heavy snow falls often provide a backcloth to the famous headlight parade around the circuit. Because of the difficult riding conditions and the need to carry a lot of equipment to keep warm, the rally is most suited to touring combinations. The classic machine to ride at the Elephant is the R75 *Wehrmachtgespann*, or their Soviet copies or the Zündapp KS 750, the original 'green elephant'. A less well-known rally, but unusual in its challenge, is the Alpine competition *In Moto Sulle Vette.* In 1981 the winners, Mario Artusio and Bruno Ciravegna, managed to ride an R100RS and an R90S to the top of Mount Chaberton, 10,298 ft (3,136 m) up the Italian Alps west of Turin. The 1:3 gravel track leading to the top is normally ice-free only for a couple of weeks at the end of August each year, and it is said to be the highest spot in the Alps to which a standard road bike can be ridden unassisted.

6

The ultimate sports machine

Since the mid-'70s BMW's connection with motorsport has been mainly in the area of car racing and the bikes rarely now appear on the circuit leader boards. Today the world's race tracks howl to the busy scream of two-strokes and the measured thud of the four-stroke engine is very rare indeed. Even chair racing, once its preserve, is now dominated by two-stroke machinery. But it was not always this way and BMW's long history is studded with sports and record achievements.

In the beginning, as now, racing was an important way to develop and sell motor cycles. Race preparation involves an urgency which sharpens ideas and speeds development changes leading to a better, more reliable product. If a bike did well on the race tracks it won public appeal and was thought likely to do as well on the road. The BMW directors soon had their early machines racing and, although the R32 never had much success on the tracks, the story altered with the development of the ohv M2B36 engines fitted to the R37 model. These specially prepared machines had a short wheelbase, nickel steel forks and light-alloy cylinder heads. Ridden by Franz Bieber, the R37 gave Munich its first national championship as early as 1924. A year later Josef Stelzer rode an R39 to win the 250 cc championship class in Germany.

Over the next five years the BMW works teams dominated road racing in Germany. The secret of their success lay with supercharging which on the fast circuits made the 500 cc and 750 cc machines almost unbeatable. A conventionally aspirated four-stroke engine works by sucking in air which is mixed with petrol, fired in the cylinder head and then exhausted as waste gases. Normally only about 95 per cent of the swept volume of each cylinder is filled on the power stroke. Supercharging works by using some of the waste gases to overcharge each cylinder by as much as 150 per cent. The full effect of the supercharging is only seen at high engine revs, but it leads to big power and torque increases. Along the fast straights the new blown racers left the opposition standing, but on the corners the better handling British bikes remained in contention. In 1927, 1928 and 1929 Paul Köppen and Ernst Henne won the tough Targa Florio race in Sicily on their 500 cc BMWs. In 1929 Henne began a remarkable series of world speed record attempts that brought him and BMW great international prestige. In 1929 his supercharged 750 cc bike developing 55 bhp reached a world speed record of 216.05 km/h (nearly 135 mph) along the autobahn near Munich. A year later he increased this record to 221.53 km/h (137.66 mph). For the next seven years he was to continue with this record breaking in Vienna, at Tat in Hungary and on the highway outside Frankfurt. Only in 1933 was the record to remain unchanged. By 1935 Henne's bike was delivering 100 bhp and he had pushed the world record to 256.046 km/h (159 mph) using comic body-streamlining aids to reduce drag. Eventually in 1936 BMW fitted a fully enclosed streamlined fairing to the flying *kompressor* and the record fell once more.

1937 was a year of motor cycle speed attempts. In April the English rider Eric Fernhough achieved 169.4 mph (272.6 km/h) on a 995 cc Brough Superior. In October a 500 cc supercharged Gilera, ridden by Piero Taruffi, the racing manager of the Gilera works team, reached 273.24 km/h (170 mph) on the Brescia to Bergamo autostrada. On November 28 near Frankfurt BMW took up the challenge and Henne, crouched low over his blown 500, pushed the record to 279.503 km/h (173.67 mph). This was Henne's 76th speed record and was not to be beaten until 1951 when Wilhelm Herz rode a 500 cc NSU to a speed of 290.3 km/h (180.39 mph).

During the 1930s, the land speed records apart, BMW motor cycles gained most of their successes in off-road and trials events. For a brief period towards the end of the decade, however, the blown 500 cc racers with double overhead cams were to be fast, reliable and victorious on the grand prix circuits. In 1936 Otto Ley won the Swedish GP on the works 500 cc machine. At the Berlin Motor Show that year H.J. Aldington, boss of AFN Ltd, the British concessionaires for BMW, and his sales manager J.M. West, convinced BMW that the racers should go to the Isle of Man for the prestigious International Tourist Trophy event. In 1937 a spring frame version *kompressor* was available and West was invited to test it at Hannover with works riders Otto Ley and Karl Gall. Jock West, despite his nickname, was born in Kent and already had a reputation as a road racer and speed trialist with Triumph and BMW machines.

In 1937 Jock made BMW's first attack on the Senior TT and won a creditable sixth place. For a while, riding the sprung BMW, he was in second place behind the Norton of Freddie Frith, the eventual winner. On the third lap the BMW coasted to a stop on Cronkny Mona hill. Jock West remembers quickly feeling for the plugs, but a numbing sensation in his lap soon confirmed a serious leak from a split tank. Fortunately the ten per cent of oil mixed in the fuel tank to lubricate the blower prevented skin burning and he was able to push it a mile to the pits, There the bike was refuelled and, despite the leak continuing, Jock managed to finish in sixth place. The bike was fast and clearly handled well and better things were soon to come. While Ley and Gall cleaned up on the European circuits Jock West won a convincing victory in the Ulster GP. This famous triangular road circuit outside Belfast included the 7.5-mile (12 km) Clady Straight, a long undulating strip of tarmac which was a gruelling ride on the unsprung machines of the day. West was to repeat his victory in 1938 and might have made it a hat-trick if a bike had been available for 1939. The 1938 race was held in very wet and windy conditions and the BMW faced stiff opposition from the Nortons of Freddie Frith and Harold Daniell. Daniell, in fact, led for eight laps but the BMW was lapping at speeds which reached 115.76 mph (186.2 km/h) along the straight. The average lap speed for the 240-mile (386 km) race was 93.98 mph (151.2 km/h) and the fastest lap of 98.93 mph (159.2 km/h) proved to be the fastest lap ever

Above *Karl Gall and Otto Ley on works 500 cc superchargers at the 1936 Swedish GP* (AFN Ltd—the W.H. Aldington collection).

Right *Ernst Henne looking thoughtful as he waits for the plugs to be changed before his 1935 record* (AFN Ltd—W.H. Aldington collection).

Below *Henne strapping on his streamlining before a 16.25-second dash along the Munich autobahn on the 750 cc supercharged BMW to a 1930 speed record of 221.53 km/h* (BMW).

Top *Henne with machine streamlining in 1936* (BMW).

Above *Jock West winning the 1937 Ulster GP on his 'blown 500'. Wet, bumpy public roads and crowds which surged at will to see the action contrast dramatically with racing conditions today* (AFN Ltd—the W.H. Aldington collection).

recorded in motor cycle road racing history. It enabled the Ulster Grand Prix to be billed as the fastest road race in Europe until the 1939 Belgium GP where Meier rode a BMW to a lap speed of 100.63 mph (161.9 km/h).

In 1938, BMW returned to the Island for another attempt on the TT but it was still not their year. Veteran rider Karl Gall crashed in practice at the Cutting (now Guthrie) and was discovered face down in a stream with a fractured skull. The works No 1 rider, Georg Meier, had to retire in the first lap with plug troubles. At the start one of the soft plugs fitted to warm up the engine seized and the mechanics were only able to fit one race plug to his machine. Jock West again rode very consistently to fifth place. Elsewhere the blown BMWs won convincingly and gave Meier and BMW the European 500 cc Championship.

A year later the BMW works team came back for its third attempt on the Isle of Man TT. The strong team included Meier, West and Gall (apparently fully recovered from his 1938 crash), a doctor and a physiotherapist. In practice the BMW *kompressors* looked and sounded good. The deep, thundrous roar of their engines was very different from the ear-splitting scream of the blown DKW two-strokes. They were clearly fast and through Crosby, probably the fastest part of the circuit, they were exceeding 130 mph (210 km/h). The flat twin layout with its low down weight seemed to have a handling advantage over the vertical singles on the twisty and bumpy track, although the heavy BMW clutch change made them slower out of corners than, for example, the Nortons. The blown twins suffered less than the singles against the strong headwinds on the Island, but Jock West remembers side gusts being a problem particularly along the Selby Straight. Some hard riding during practice signalled the Germans' intention to win this time. The unfortunate Gall, however, crashed again this time at Ballaugh. He was taken to Ramsey hospital where Dr Bergerman operated but he died from his serious head injuries. His two team mates got little sleep that night but next morning they were persuaded to carry on.

On his first leg of the race Meier averaged over 90 mph (145 km/h) from a standing start. The two BMWs led for all four laps with only Stan Woods on the Velocette and Freddie Frith's Norton still in contention at the finish. Georg Meier's win was the first by a foreigner in the Senior TT, then the most highly-prized trophy in motor cycle racing. Meier's winning race time was 2 hours 57 minutes 19 seconds which was an average of 89.38 mph (143.8 km/h). This just failed to equal the lap record of 91 mph (146 km/h) set a year earlier on a Manx Norton by Harold Daniell.

The full story of the bikes used by the BMW works team to win the 1939 Senior TT has still to be told but it is evidently rich in rumour and intrigue. Officially the power output of the super-charged racers was given as 56 bhp, but their performance on the day has produced guesstimates ranging between 50 and 100 bhp. At the official weigh in after the race Meier's machine turned the scales at 302 lb (137 kg) making it the lightest bike in the field. This compares with a standard 500 cc (R51) machine which weighed 400 lb (182 kg). Jock West's bike weighed 307 lb but, having ridden both machines, he remains convinced that his was identical to the one ridden by Meier. Despite the German reputation for strict adherence to the rules, team control was informal enough to let Jock West carry out some modifications to the bikes. In order to make some extra start money, West used Lodge plugs, Dunlop tyres and even fitted a Dunlop-made saddle. At the time Meier saw this financial fettling as highly amusing as, for most of the race, neither rider remained in his saddle long before sliding on to the rear extension pad. Some controversy also surrounds the question of whether Meier's bike was fitted with balanced brakes or whether this was only a feature of the German GP. The facts are that Meier had had a balanced braking system fitted to all his bikes following an injury to his wrist during a three-day mountain race in 1934.

On August 6 1939 the BMW bikes were in Sweden at the Saxtorp Grand Prix. Battling with Dorini Serafini, the Italian ace on a blown Gilera, Meier fell, remounted and fell again. His injuries prevented further racing that season and ruined his expectation of retaining the European Championship. Other spills in practice played havoc with the team bikes which probably numbered five, and BMW found themselves unable to offer Jock West a works ride for his third attack on the Ulster. This may, however, have been a tactful way for BMW to react to the knowledge that Germany was about to launch a different sort of attack of its own in the first week of September!

During the Second World War the BMW racing bikes were stored in Munich and motor cycle production was directed to military applications only. One of the *kompressors* is said to have turned up in France after the Liberation and it may be significant that Georg Meier served for some time in Paris. Another of the racing bikes which escaped the bombing of Munich is said to have been looted by a Russian General who knew its value but not how to handle it and rider and machine came to a sudden end against a brick wall. Despite the damage to the BMW factories and the widespread appropriation of spoils of war by the Allies, the 500 cc supercharged racers miraculously re-appeared in the grey aftermath of the war.

Meier was soon back in the saddle and with fellow works rider, Ludwig 'Wiggerl' Kraus, began a domination of the re-awakening German road racing scene. Elsewhere in the world supercharging had been outlawed in 1946, but German motor sport did not regain international recognition until 1950. For the next three years Meier and his pupil Walter Zeller raced and developed naturally-aspirated racers using the first BMW pivot suspension. By the 1953 season the BMW Rennsport was pivoted front and rear and was using a 60 bhp fuel injection engine. The last solo version of the Rennsport appeared with an improved frame for the 1956 season. Meier, Zeller and Ernst Hiller won a number of national races on this RS model 256 and Zeller was runner up in the 500 cc Championship to John Surtees. A

The official caption to this photograph describes it simply as 'Jock West at speed at Governor's Bridge during practice on the TT Course'. In fact the story is far more detailed and poignant. Jock, riding No 49, borrowed from Meier because his own machine was being stripped, is returning from Ballagh where team mate Karl Gall had sustained a fractured skull crashing his bike. Gall's damaged helmet can be seen hanging from Jock West's back. The scene is evocative of the highest levels of comradeship which team sport can generate (Jock West).

Above left and right *Georg 'Schorsch' Meier still riding at Schotten in 1951 and still riding at Creg-Ny-Bass on the Millenium lap of Honour in the 1979 Isle of Man TT* (BMW/Chris Kitts).

Below *Walter Zeller on the fuel-injection Rennmaschine in 1953* (BMW).

works ride in the 1956 Senior TT did not, however, recapture the pre-war supremacy of the BMW racers. Other famous racers of the time tried to put the BMW through its paces and in 1958 ex-Gilera star Geoff Duke won on one at Hockenheim. One of the best efforts was by privateer Dickie Dale who gave BMW third place in the 500 cc World Championships of 1958 behind the MV Agusta team of Surtees and Hartle. At this time the 500 cc MV machines were giving over 65 bhp and were capable of speeds of up to 150 mph (240 km/h). At GP level the solo BMW was not able to compete with such sheer power and the works support was withdrawn in company with Gilera and Moto Guzzi. The MVs in the hands of superstars such as Surtees (500 cc World Champion 1956, 1958-60), Mike Hailwood (1962-5), Giacomo Agostini (1966-72) and Phil Read (1972-4) were left to dominate the 350 cc and 500 cc classes in road racing.

Instead, the RS was to make its mark in sidecar racing where its domination of the world championships was to be even more complete than MV's occupation of the 500 cc class. BMW *beiwagen* or sidecar outfits had been raced before the Second World War but mostly by private entrants. In 1936 a works team was formed with Stelzer and Kraus and a 600 cc supercharged engine. Typical of the versatility of riders in those days, the same Stelzer and Kraus along with Henne, Müller and Mauermeyer had just completed a hat-trick of International Six Day Events wins on BMW machinery. Later, after the war, chairs were raced using R51 and R75 engines. By 1952 there were two works teams consisting of Ludwig Kraus and Bernard Huser and Wilhelm Noll and Fritz Cron. It was the latter who were to start the long run of world sidecar championships for BMW. In 1954 they finally wrested the title from Eric Oliver and Stan Dibben and their indomitable Norton combination. Now it was the BMW twin that was to prove invincible.

The RS motor proved ideal for sidecar racing with its broad power range and low-slung layout. It was also the time when BMW was fitting Earles-type suspension to their bikes and this was found preferable to telescopic forks for fully-faired outfits. The strong engine produced 60 bhp at 9,500 rpm and this gave the BMW outfits a very competitive edge on the opposition. On October 29 1954 Noll used the 500 cc RS engine to set a world speed record of between 106-115 mph (171-185 km/h) for an hour at the famous Montlhéry speed track near Paris. Earlier in May, at the same circuit, Georg Meier and his brother Hans along with Walter Zeller had ridden a solo RS to a world speed record of 103.7 mph (166.6 km/h) over eight and nine hours. For 20 years the BMW *Werksgespann* notched up success after success in sidecar racing. Between 1955 and 1972 only once did BMW let slip their stranglehold on the Isle of Man TT sidecar championship when Chris Vincent won on a BSA outfit. In 1962 Max Deubel broke all the previous sidecar speed records at the Isle of Man TT when he achieved a 90 mph (145 km/h) lap. In the 1969 race BMW outfits took six of the first seven places. Between 1954 and 1974 the World Championship and Constructors Team Prizes were won 19 times in succession by BMW. The only serious competition came from the URS, a unique 500 cc four with a double overhead cam, which was the design of Helmut Fath and named after his home town of Ursenbach. Fath had raced for BMW in 1960 but crashed at the Nürburgring where he lost his right foot and his passenger, Alfred Wohlgemut, was killed. On 12 occasions in the 13 years before the URS arrived on the scene BMW outfits took the first three places in the World Championship.

The days of the four-stroke racer were numbered, however, and the light but immensely powerful two-stroke machines began crowding the starting grids. A BMW works team continued until 1976 when Mike Krauser put together a beautiful-looking, fuel-injected Rennsport to try to beat off

Max Klankermeier and Hermann Wolz on a works outfit. This pair dominated chair racing in Germany in 1948 and 1949. A filmstar, Hans Albers, is riding pillion! (BMW).

the two-stroke superiority. FIM noise restriction regulations limited its power to 75 bhp which was not enough then to remain competitive. Thus, for a while at least, ended BMW's active participation in road racing motor cycles.

Meantime back at the record tracks Noll, Friedrich Hillebrand and Walter Schneider had ridden an RS outfit for 24 hours in March 1955 at an average speed of almost 90 mph (144.3 km/h). The last official works record run was on the autobahn near Munich on October 5 1955. First Zeller rode a solo RS at an average speed of 150 mph (241.8 km/h) for a distance of 10 miles. Shortly afterwards Noll piloted a totally-enclosed RS sidecar running on nitromethane and alcohol to a flying start speed of 174.13 mph (280.22 km/h).

In 1959 the 24-hour record was pushed up to 95.6 (153.9 km/h) by a French team consisting of Rene Vasseur, Robert Maucherat, Alain Dagan and Claude Lariviere. March 1961 saw this 24-hour record change twice in one week as Montlhéry's bumpy concrete resounded to the continuous roar of the four-stroke record-breakers.

First the French rider, Georges Monneret on a Velocette Venom set fresh records for 12 and 24 hours endurance riding. Then a British racing team, MLG, took over the track and promptly rewrote the record book. Riders Ellis Boyce, George Catlin, John Holder and Sid Mizen rode an R69S for 12 hours at an average speed of 109.34 mph (175.96 km/h) and 24 hours at 109.24 mph (175.8 km/h) including all pit stops. The R69S had a factory-prepared engine and megaphone exhausts. Esso Petroleum helped

Left *Ludwig 'Wiggerl' Kraus and Bernhard Huser, winners of the 1951 German GP* (BMW).

Below *Klaus Enders and Ralf Engelhardt show their pace at the Brands Hatch Hutchinson 100, August 9 1970. The pair won six world championships between 1967 and 1974* (Motor Cycle Weekly).

sponsor the attempt during which the bike consumed eight tyres, one at the front and seven on the rear! There was hardly a problem for the whole period of the record attempt, although within five minutes of the finish a thick mist came down and shrouded the track. The same bike, minus its Peel fairing, was later road tested by *Motor Cycling* magazine and found to have a top speed of 118 mph (190 km/h).

MLG was a BMW dealership in West London and had been preparing BMW motor cycles for racing since 1958. At Thruxton in that year MLG entered an R50 borrowed from a regular customer in the 500 mile endurance race. The bike was absolutely road standard yet purred into third place against the deafening roar of the Triumphs. The team quickly learnt that production racing was about fettling and racing modifications. For the 1959 race at Thruxton they prepared an R69 with a deep sump, special carburettors, a big tank, air scoops on the front brakes, a mechanical rev counter and skids for the exposed rocker covers. The bike was ridden by Bruce Daniels and John Lewis and won the race. The same year saw the MLG team of four mechanics and two riders at the famous Montjuich circuit outside Barcelona. Here Bruce Daniels and Peter Darvill took on the mighty Ducati works team in the 24-hour endurance race. Despite the shoestring budget the BMW dominated the race. Overnight the spectators always knew when the BMW was coming by the dancing display of sparks as the cambox skids negotiated the winding circuit. Two years later the BMW, this time with Peter Darvill and Norman Price riding, again won the 24-hour race. Later that year it was also successful in the Silverstone 1,000 km marathon. Soon afterwards MLG withdrew from racing activities. As frequently happens with dealer sponsorship, the time comes when the costs of racing interfere with the running of the business and the team gets disbanded.

The most powerful BMW racers ever were the highly-modified R90S production bikes run by Butler & Smith in the '70s when they were BMW concessionaires for the USA. Modifications to these bikes involved stiffening the frame, changing the suspension, fitting a new clutch and gearbox, adding Mikuni carburettors and using specially shortened connecting rods and pistons to reduce engine width and improve cornering clearance. In full trim these machines were producing up to 50 per cent more power than the standard R90S which itself was good for 125 mph (200 km/h). Power output on the R75/7 engine

MLG's Thruxton 500 (Alf Cook, MLG).

was pushed from 50 to 82 bhp by similar modifications. Best known of the riders for this flamboyant race team was British-born Reg Pridmore who now runs a BMW dealership in California. The most successful year of the team was in 1974 when the BMWs won the American Motor Cycle Association Superbike Championship. In the 1974 Daytona Reg Pridmore, riding a BMW with a Rob North frame, came in 37th, the second four-stroke home after a Harley-Davidson. It was the same year that the first Yamaha TZ750s arrived to confirm the two-stroke takeover of the world's race tracks.

Production and endurance racing have helped to keep some BMW motor cycles on the racing circuits in the '70s. Helmut Dahne, a development rider for Metzeler Tyres, has been a popular visitor to the Isle of Man TT races on his specially prepared R90/S. In 1973 the Gus Kuhn Racing Team won the production class at Barcelona with an experimental R75/5. Development work by the factory had increased power output by 30 per cent and the bike was fitted with twin front discs and a five-speed box. The riders were Dave Potter and Graham Sharpe. The Gus Kuhn Racing Team started in 1968 and for nearly a decade competed at virtually all the British circuits including the Isle of Man, plus many of the continental events. The team included Nortons and BMWs and, in 1975, involved some sponsorship from *Penthouse* magazine. Eventually the heavy expenses of modern road racing forced an end to the team. It was also clear that the BMW could not really compete in endurance racing as it is today. Big factory entrants have made events such as the Bol D'Or and the 24-hour at Barcelona very professional and competitive. With works support

Above *Reg Pridmore aboard a racing R90S with Rob North frame in the 1974 Daytona. This 90 bhp special weighed a mere 310 lb (141 kg)* (Motor Cycle Weekly).

Below *The Gus Kuhn Racing Team R75/5 developed with BMW support. Team manager, Vincent Davey, discusses fairing changes with Hans-Gunther von der Marwitz, BMW's development engineer, while rider, Dave Potter, watches team mechanic, Dave Sleat's, right hand!* (BMW GB).

on a massive scale these events have been transformed from competitions of endurance and reliability into 24-hour races. BMW cannot match the Japanese factories in their commitment to this form of racing. Against such highly-developed machines the BMW has insufficient power and its gearbox is not strong enough to stand long hours of racing changes. It remains to be seen whether BMW's current development programme can once again produce a competitive racing machine. A powerful, water-cooled square four with better ground clearance and an improved gearbox might form the basis of a successful works team.

For the moment the BMW motor cycle racing budget remains tiny compared with the company's commitment to motorsport. Works support is devoted almost entirely to off-road racing where BMW have the best chance of being successful. The R80 G/S prototypes have proved a large but potent force in international trials events and works support has brought victories in cross-country races such as the Paris-Dakar. It carries on a tradition which goes all the way back to the early Six Days rides by Rudolf Schleicher on the R37 and BMW wins in gruelling road races such as the Targa Florio.

At first sight BMWs do not look the part for off-road sport but, as the record shows, the famous white and blue emblem has featured in every form of motor cycle sport from hill trials to ice racing. The most famous of the international endurance competitions is the International Six Days Event, an annual trial that has been run since 1913. Competitors cover about 150 miles a day over rough cross-country routes with timed stages and speed sections. Overnight the machines are secured and no part, except tyres, may be changed during the whole competition. The lightness and mechanical simplicity of two-strokes make them an obvious choice for such a test and certainly the most consistently successful teams have come from factories such as MZ, Zündapp, Puch,

Bultaco and more recently Kawasaki, Suzuki and Yamaha. BMW dependability has, however, frequently brought Vase and Trophy wins to the works team. The early British domination of the International Six Days Trophy was first broken in 1933 when the German BMW team won by a single point on specially prepared R16 machines. The following year the event was held at Garmish-Partenkirchen and the BMW team on R4 models won two gold medals.

One of motor cycle sport's most dramatic moments took place in 1939 when the ISDE teams gathered for the 21st time at Salzburg a few days before the outbreak of the Second World War. Korpsfuhrer Huhnlein, the Reich's sports minister, had promised all those taking part a safe passage to the nearest frontier in the event of hostilities. It was an odd replay of the circumstances surrounding the 1914 event when the teams had been trapped in Grenoble, France, as a world war began. Britain was represented at Salzburg by an Army team mounted on BSA and Norton bikes. The competition was between Britain, Germany and Italy for the International Trophy. By the end of the fifth day the political situation had become so serious that the British team withdrew from the competition and raced for the security of the Swiss border. The German team on BMW and DKW machines duly won the Trophy while the Silver Vase went to the BMW-mounted German 'A' team. A personal moment of drama in this situation is recalled by Jock West who was a spectator at Salzburg with his wife as guests of BMW. Unable to provide him with a bike for the 1939 Ulster, BMW had loaned Jock a car for a short holiday in southern Germany. In the ensuing chaos of general mobilisation, travel restrictions and petrol shortages the Wests found themselves with a German registered car 138 km from the way home. Fritz Trötsch, a BMW competitions manager who had, ironically, himself been a prisoner of war on the Isle of Man during the First World War, had to work quickly to get them back to Munich and on the last 'plane to England. The lunacy of war now interrupted motor cycle sport in Europe for seven years. Jock West and Georg Meier, having been in the same team for BMW, now found themselves in opposing teams. Back in England Jock West joined the RAF and eventually reached the rank of Wing Commander and was awarded the OBE.

After the war BMW off-road machinery evolved slowly, mostly in the hands of privateers such as Herbert Schek, a BMW dealer in Wangen, South Germany. He began using an R50, complete

Above *Hubert Auriol aviates the R80 G/S in the 1981 Paris–Dakar with a group of Tuaregs admiring his style* (BMW).

Below *Richard Schalber putting the suspension of his GS80 to a severe test* (BMW).

with Earles forks, for scrambles and enduro events back in 1960. BMW enduro success has come mostly in the over 500 cc class and with sidecars where the two-stroke advantages tend to even out. In 1978 the factory returned officially to competition work and in 1979 the prototype of the current R80 G/S model triumphed in the ISDE. A 57 bhp GS 80, ridden by Fritz Witzel, won the 750 cc class outright. In 1980 Rolf Witthöff won the over 500 cc European Enduro Championship and went on to win a gold medal at the International Trophy event in France. In 1981 the factory once more withdrew from the ISDE claiming the competition had lost its publicity value and that complex regulations now made things too difficult for the modest racing budget available. This type of racing has, however, helped to prove some of the notable BMW motor cycle design advances. In 1935 the ISDE gave the supercharged engines the ultimate trial and the off-road successes of the R4 model must have helped convince the German Army of its military potential. Enduro experience has also clearly convinced the factory that monoshock suspension systems, first developed in the mid-'70s, could be used to create the unique monolever suspension fitted to the R80 G/S dual purpose model.

Technical specification of the GS 80

Engine: Flat twin four-stroke. 870 cc (95 mm × 61.5 mm). Compression ratio 9.8:1. **Claimed output:** 57 bhp. Two 32 mm Bing carburettors. **Ignition:** Pointless electronic. **Transmission:** Five-speed gearbox with light Fitchel & Sachs single plate clutch. **Suspension:** Duplex frame in 1 mm chrome-molybdenum tubing. Maico air-assisted forks with 10.2 in (260 mm) travel. Swinging arm with Bilstein gas damper giving 9.6 in (245 mm) travel. **Brakes:** Front 6 in (150 mm) single leading shoe. Rear 8 in (200 mm). **Weight:** 308 lb (140 kg) with fuel and tools. Tank holds 2.2 gallons (10 litres). **Tyres:** 3.00—21 at front and 5.00—17 at rear. One bike is preserved in the BMW Museum in Munich.

Moto-cross racing is a shorter but more furious version of the ISDE competition. The circuits normally present every riding surface problem possible and winning lies in rider/machine handling rather than sheer speed and power. This form of racing began in England in 1924 and has since become very popular on the continent. Originally the 500 cc class was dominated by AJS, BSA and Norton singles, but since the mid-'60s the two-stroke machines have had it all their own way. It takes some muscle and considerable courage to force a BMW up a slippery gully or off a steep slope, but the German Moto-Cross Championships have been won regularly by the Bavarian twins. One of the best known riders and a frequent captain of the German ISDE team is Sebastian Nachtmann, a bike dealer in Munich. Since the formation of the bigger classes in moto-cross, the European Championship has been won several times by BMW works specials. In 1980, for example, Herbert Schek won the 1,000 cc class.

After the Second World War R75 outfits were raced in off-road competition especially in Germany and, in the 1960s, the R69S engine often powered the chairs. Since then the BMW sidecars have been more of a rarity for off-road use. Thus it was a surprise for British fans in 1974 when the Hughenden Moto-Cross outfit appeared on the scene. Hughenden was a BMW car dealership in High Wycombe and the idea of racing off-road belonged to sales manager Ron Slater. Slater was then in the process of establishing the BMW motor cycle franchise now familiar as Hughenden M40. The outfit was raced by Terry Good and Jess Rixon who later became British Moto-Cross Champions. The team gained more in publicity than from success largely because the BMW transmission was not designed for the abuses of moto-cross racing. In 1976 the outfit was converted to grass track racing and fitted with a specially tuned R90S engine. The plot ridden by Roger and Jeff Measor raced for six successive seasons successfully demonstrating the versatility and reliability of BMW engineering. It attracted much attention at meetings in Britain and on the continent because of its novelty, the originality shown in its development and the immaculateness of its appearance in the BMW motorsport colours of pink, mauve and blue on a white background. The later version used a 750 cc block with a 14:1 compression ratio, Venolia pistons, a sports camshaft, 40 mm Dell'Orto carburettors with methanol fuel and electronic ignition with two plugs per cylinder and produced over 9,000 rpm on full song. The 90 odd bhp was driven through a standard BMW gearbox with a Formula 3 car racing clutch and a drive shaft modified from a BMW 2002 saloon. Open pipes were necessary to retain top end power and a major problem before each race was to pass the scrutiny of the noise regulations.

Long distance rallying has always been recognised by car manufacturers as a useful test of all-round reliability and dependability and it is appropriate that the main BMW effort now is in supporting such events. Currently the most popular of these events is the Paris—Dakar Rally which involves crossing the Sahara desert and stretches man and machine to the limits. The Paris—Dakar was first run in 1979 and the route runs some 6,200 miles (10,000 km) from the capital of France to the capital of Senegal in West Africa. The race for cars and bikes is run over 20 one-day stages in January when the desert is coolest. The real test comes from nearly 2,000 miles (3,200 km) of off-road riding across sand and rocky tracks subject to intense heat, dust storms, sudden flash floods and the unpredictable traffic manners of Bedouin camels, goats and roosters.

The 1981 race was won by the French BMW team of Hubert Auriol (first), Jean-Claude Fenouil (fourth) and Bernard Neimer (seventh). 101 motor cycles and 130 cars, including a Rolls-Royce, took part and there were also works teams from Honda and Yamaha. The 20-day battle was prepared for like a military operation. The BMW back-up team included three Puch cross-country vehicles with mechanics and tools to cope with any emergency. These specialists were nicknamed the 'Desert Foxes' and included Dr Helmut Pohl, responsible for BMW's sports activities. The bikes were specially prepared R80 G/S machines fitted with long-range tanks and strengthened frames. A particular adaptation was the fitting of a high level air filter built into the tank. Although considerably heavier than the competition, the strong boxer motors proved suitably flexible in the difficult conditions. The fact that shaft drive BMWs rise under initial acceleration proved to be a bonus for getting out of deep sand conditions.

Auriol, known affectionately as *Der Afrikaner*, finished three hours ahead of the second machine to finish, an XT 500. This 28-year-old textile salesman was born in Ethiopia and was a trials champion in 1977, 1978 and 1979. Fenouil, a biking journalist, and desert veteran, was the first motor cycle rider to cross the Sahara Desert alone in 1973. In 1978 he created a record of 12 hours and 34 minutes for a trans-Saharan bike ride of over 900 miles (1,450 km) between Algiers and Tamanrasset. Neimer is already an old hand on the Paris—Dakar, having come second in 1979. When he is not racing he is in charge of a Paris police motor cycle squad. The 1981 race also included Herbert Schek and Karl Frederick Capito on their own bikes sponsored by BMW. Only 25 of the motor cycle starters eventually made it to the finish in Dakar.

Endurance races such as the Paris—Dakar clearly demonstrate that any bike which will stand up to such a degree of concentrated outrage must find everyday use well within its capacity. A win helps a manufacturer sell bikes because buyers will take pride in knowing that they have a world-beating model. The reality, of course, is that intense competition between manufacturers means that they can ill afford to leave things to chance in such events and these racing machines are much modified from those available in the showrooms.

	Paris—Dakar R80 G/S	***Production R80 G/S***
Engine	4-stroke flat twin	
Capacity	798 cc	798 cc
Bore × Stroke	84.8 × 70.6 mm	84.8 × 70.6 mm
Claimed output	55 bhp	50 bhp
Compression ratio	9.5:1	8.2:1
Carburettors	2/32 mm Bing	2/32 mm Bing
Transmission	5-speed gears with dry single plate clutch	
Brakes	Front disc with rear drum	
Front tyre	3.25-21	3.00-21
Rear tyre	5.00-17	4.00-18
Front fork travel	270 mm	200 mm
Rear damper travel	240 mm	170 mm
Wheelbase	1,555 mm	1,465 mm
All up weight	150 kg	186 kg
Fuel Tank	42 litres	19.5 litres

One rather special event where the whole point of the exercise is to demonstrate outstanding reliability in a standard machine is the Maudes Trophy, and BMW has been the holder since 1973. The Trophy has only been awarded 15 times since it was first presented by the Auto Cycle Union in the 1920s. In May 1973 two standard Stroke 5 750 cc machines were brought direct from the factory production line and started on a week of lapping the difficult 37¾-mile (60.7 km) TT circuit on the Isle of Man. The test was to maintain an average speed of 50 mph (80 km/h) which meant lapping every 45 minutes. There were 15 riders in the team and BMW Concessionaires (GB) provided the support services. The riders included journalists such as Bruce Preston, one of the founder members of the BMW Club of Great Britain, and dealers like Tony Jefferies from Sheffield who was an experienced TT rider. Despite several accidents in the low cloud and rain that shrouded the mountain part of the circuit for most of the week, the challenge was realised. One bike clocked 8,490 miles (13,663 km) at an average speed of 50.47 mph (81.26 km/h) and the other completed 217 laps at an average speed of 48.68 mph (78 km/h).

No major mechanical faults developed over the week but one machine did receive some spirited attention from BMW service manager, Alberto Criscuolo. Following a tumble the bike came to a halt after Glen Helen with a seized clutch. Carbon tetrachloride from a fire extinguisher was enough to free the plates, but the clutch was found to slip badly. The imaginative Italian got the disabled bike back to the service point by borrowing a bottle of brandy from a nearby inn and emptying the contents on the clutch to make it sticky! For a while there was some speculation that this unusual technique might subsequently be incorporated in revisions to BMW service manuals. The award of the Trophy was a fitting reward for a remarkable achievement and appropriately marked the 50th anniversary of the flat twin design. Here was clear proof that the original Max Friz concept of dependable, strong and long-living motor cycles was alive and well.

The BMW sporting heritage is a proud record of consistency and staying power. Appropriately, the strength of the machines has invariably been matched by their riders. At the time it seemed difficult to imagine matching American John Penton's epic ride on an R69 from New York to Los Angeles in just over 52 hours. The trip of 3,051 miles (4,909 km) was covered at an average speed of nearly 60 mph (96 km/h) and the indefatigable Penton took only three hours sleep. Yet 21 years later an R80 G/S is guided halfway across the world in only 18 days. This 10,000-mile trip (16,000 km) involved crossing the busiest part of Europe, an excitable Middle East and a 3,500-mile (5,600 km) haul across the lonely Nullabar Plain. Here the determination of rider and machine was even able to withstand a collision with a jaywalking kangaroo! The trip was to prove an idea, something which BMW's racing and record breaking activities have made a continuing tradition.

Highlights from BMW's motor cycle racing achievements

Solos

1924 German 500 cc National Road Championship, Franz Bieber.
1925 German GP, Paul Köppen, 500 cc.
1926 German GP, Josef Stelzer, 500 cc.
1927 German GP, Josef Stelzer, 750 cc. Austrian GP, Emmerich Nagy, 500 cc. Luxembourg GP, Josef Stelzer, 1,000 cc. Targa Florio, Paul Köppen, 500 cc.
1928 Austrian GP, Karl Gall, 1,000 cc. Targa Florio, Ernst Henne, 500 cc.
1929 Polish GP, Adolf Brudes, over 500 cc. Austrian GP, Otto Steinfellner, 1,000 cc. Targa Florio, Paul Köppen, 500 cc.
1930 German GP, Fritz Wiese, 1,000 cc. Hungarian GP, Karl Stegmann, 500 cc.
1931 Hungarian GP, Michael Culyba, 600 cc.
1933 German GP, Josef Stelzer, 500 cc. German GP, Eduard Kratz, 1,000 cc.
1936 Swedish GP, Otto Ley, 500 cc.
1937 German GP, Karl Gall, 500 cc. Dutch TT, Karl Gall, 500 cc. Ulster GP, Jock West, 500 cc. Hungarian GP, Karl Gall, 500 cc. Swedish GP, Otto Ley, 500 cc.
1938 German GP, Georg Meier, 500 cc. Dutch TT, Georg Meier, 500 cc. Belgian GP, Georg Meier, 500 cc. Italian GP, Georg Meier, 500 cc. Ulster GP, Jock West, 500 cc. Rumanian GP, Ludwig Kraus, 500 cc.
1939 English TT, Georg Meier, 500 cc. Dutch TT, Georg Meier, 500 cc. Belgian GP, Georg Meier, 500 cc. Rumanian GP, Ludwig Kraus, 500 cc.
1950 German GP, Walter Zeller, 500 cc.
1953 German GP, Walter Zeller, 500 cc.
1956 Czechoslovakian GP, Gerold Klinger, 500 cc.
1957 Czechoslovakian GP, Gerold Klinger, 500 cc.
1958 East German GP, Richard Dale, 500 cc.
1958 Czechoslovakian GP, Richard Dale, 500 cc.
1958 Austrian GP, Ernst Hiller, 500 cc.

Sidecar world championships

1954 Wilhelm Noll/Fritz Cron.
1955 Willi Faust/Karl Remmert.
1956 Wilhelm Noll/Fritz Cron.
1957 Friedrich Hillebrand/Manfred Grunwald.
1958 Walter Schneider/Hans Strauss.
1959 Walter Schneider/Hans Strauss.
1960 Helmut Fath/Alfred Wohlgemut.
1961 Max Deubel/Emil Hörner.
1962 Max Deubel/Emil Hörner.
1963 Max Deubel/Emil Hörner.
1964 Max Deubel/Emil Hörner.
1965 Fritz Scheidegger/John Robinson.
1966 Fritz Scheidegger/John Robinson.
1967 Klaus Enders/Ralf Engelhardt.
1969 Klaus Enders/Ralf Engelhardt.
1970 Klaus Enders/Ralf Engelhardt.
1972 Klaus Enders/Ralf Engelhardt.
1973 Klaus Enders/Ralf Engelhardt.
1974 Klaus Enders/Ralf Engelhardt.

World records

1929 September 9: Ernst Henne on a 750 cc at Munich—flying kilometre at 134.25 mph (216.050 km/h).
1930 September 20: Ernst Henne on a 750 cc at Munich—flying kilometre at 137.66 mph (221.53 km/h).
1931 September: Ernst Henne on a 750 cc solo and a 750 cc sidecar in Vienna—speeds of 148.08 mph (238.3 km/h) and 118.58 mph (190.83 km/h).

Helmut Dahne, a Metzeler tyre tester and Isle of Man specialist banks his R90S. Dahne has been one of the most consistent post-war BMW privateers (BMW).

1932 November 3: Ernst Henne on a 750 cc at Tat—flying kilometre at 151.87 mph (244.399 km/h).

1934 October 10: Ernst Henne on a 750 cc at Tat—flying kilometre at 152.9 mph (246.059 km/h).

1935 September 27: Ernst Henne on a 750 cc at Frankfurt—flying kilometre at 159.1 mph (256.046 km/h).

1936 October 12: Ernst Henne on a 500 cc at Frankfurt—flying kilometre at 169.02 mph (272.006 km/h).

1937 November 28: Ernst Henne on a 500 cc at Frankfurt—flying kilometre at 173.68 mph (279.503 km/h).

1954 May 12: Georg and Hans Meier with Walter Zeller set a nine-hour record of 103.55 mph (166.64 km/h) at Montlhéry in the 500 cc class. On October 30 Willhelm Noll rode a 500 cc at the same track over 10 km at 132.17 mph (212.7 km/h).

1955 October 3: Wilhelm Noll, Fritz Hillebrand and Walter Schneider rode a sidecar at Montlhéry for 24 hours at average of 89.67 mph (144.3 km/h). Two days later Walter Zeller pushed the 10 km solo record to 150.25 mph (241.8 km/h) and Noll took the sidecar over 1 km at 174.13 mph (280.22 km/h).

1961 March 3: Sid Mizen, George Catlin, John Holder and Ellis Boyce of the MLG team rode an R69S at Montlhéry to a 12- and 24-hour record of 109.36 mph (176 km/h).

7

The Bayerische Motoren Werke AG—Munich

Munich, an exciting cultural centre and capital for Bavaria, is also the largest centre for industry and business in the southern part of Federal Germany. For 64 years it has been home town to the Bayerische Motoren Werke and the fortunes of BMW have been very much the fortunes of Munich. This city is famous for many specialities. Its attractions range from the fascinations within its museums and galleries through the culinary delights of *Schweinshaxen* (roast knuckle of pork) to the heady atmosphere of its noted beer halls. One speciality which the whole world has come to appreciate is the output of one of its most progressive industrial concerns, BMW AG.

A visitor to BMW's distinctive headquarters off the Petuelring overlooking Munich's Olympia Park is instantly made aware that this is no ordinary company. The four gleaming cylinders towering against the Munich skyline are brilliantly symbolic of the quality and presence which the world has come to associate with BMW's products. The image fits a company with an annual turnover in 1980 of nearly 7,000 million DM. The amazing tower block, known locally as the *Vierzylinder*, houses the administration. On a clear day its 1,000 blue-tinted windows react with the silver-clad structure to beam the company colours across the city. Not that this is really necessary as Munich is very much a company town and the white and blue logo adorns a great number of offices, factory complexes and showrooms. Indeed, with over 18,000 employees in Munich alone, the BMW offices and plants very nearly form an urban community in themselves. There are BMW health clinics, catering establishments, a training college, a computer complex, a postal service, bus and taxi operations and even a museum, art gallery and archive centre.

BMW began in somewhat humbler surroundings just one of several brick factories on the edge of Munich's airfield in the suburbs of the city. Here the founding fathers, Karl Rapp and

BMW AG Munich. Once on the outskirts of Munich the BMW head-office and car plant are surrounded by housing and the Olympia Park with its radio mast (BMW).

Max Friz, ran the Bayerische Flugzeugwerke AG. Its exclusive product was engines and its speciality was high-altitude versions. On August 13 1918 the company took its present name, the Bayerische Motoren Werke AG. It employed 3,500 workers and had a stock capital of 12 million RM. The company got off to a shaky start as Germany's defeat in the First World War brought aero engine production to a halt. Substitute production was found in farm equipment and railway castings before the possibilities of motor cycle manufacture began to be exploited. The first production line for the R32 bike was set up in a corner of the old BFW factory on Leichenauer Road and over a four-year period produced over 4,000 machines. Considerable publicity had been won for the new design following the bike's exhibition at the 1923 Paris Motor Show. By the mid-'20s BMW was well established as a company. There were nine models in its motor cycle range and the production of aeroplane engines was in full swing again. The 1920s were a boom period for motor cycle sales and Germany had several volume manufacturers which included DKW, NSU and Zündapp. BMW produced about 3 per cent of the total German output of motor bikes, but it was all at the top end of the market and included exports to countries such as Denmark and Sweden. The Zündapp company in Nuremberg, which switched to motor cycle manufacture at about the same time as BMW, produced its 100,000th machine in 1933 five years before BMW reached that volume.

One effect of the Golden '20s was to persuade the German public that four-wheeled vehicles had a number of advantages over bikes, and thus the demand for cars took off. BMW gambled on expansion and bought a car factory at Eisenach some 440 km north of Munich. This plant had been in the vehicle business since 1896, at first building bicycles and electric cars and more recently French Decauvilles under the trade name of Wartburg, a local castle. Years later this name was to reappear on a two-stroke car produced by the other Germany. In 1928 the Eisenach factory was producing British-designed Austin 7 cars and the sale to BMW included the licence to continue manufacture of this small four-cylinder car renamed the Dixi.

Thus, at the end of its first ten years, BMW appeared a strong and well-balanced company. The R62, the first 750 cc motor cycle, was ready for release and 25,000 BMW bikes were on the roads of Europe including Britain where BMW had already exhibited at Olympia. On the aero-

engine side the Mk VI, a liquid-cooled V-12 engine, which was to remain in series production until the Second World War, was attracting the world's aviation authorities by its record-breaking achievements. To this was now added motor car manufacture. It had meant heavy borrowing from the banks but the investment looked secure in a Germany enjoying, since 1924, something of an economic revival. Warning signs were there, however, and even a well-established company such as NSU at Neckarsulm, which had been in business since 1873 and building cars since 1905, was forced to suspend production and sell off some of its facilities to Fiat of Italy.

Company expansionism suddenly seemed to be a mistake. 1929 was the year of the world stock market crash and, with inflation racing away, BMW found itself committed to marketing the 3/15, a modified Dixi and to be known affectionately as the 'Flea'. Despite the doom and gloom of the recession BMW went ahead, stepped up production and increased the payroll to 3,860. Dividends were halved and the bank loan was doubled, but the company now seemed set to see its future as firmly established on four wheels as it had previously been on two. The heavy investment in cars did, however, stretch BMW's resources to the limit and at the beginning of the '30s its surging growth hiccuped. Over a two-year period turnover dropped, dividends ceased and half the staff were shed. In March 1930 BMW made delivery of its 1,000th Mk VI engine. The big bikes were not selling well because of their prices, which then, as now, represented almost half the annual income of typical working people. Recently introduced taxation legislation in Germany did promote the sales of under 200 cc motor cycles and BMW bowed to the inevitable and rushed a 'tax-free' model into production. The 198 cc R2 did not save the company in any real sense, but it undoubtedly helped with cash flow problems, as did the R4 which won a worthwhile Army contract on the basis of its cross-country capability. For a second time motor cycles could be said to be securing the company's survival and by 1933 things were on course again.

During the '30s the sporting and record achievements in the air, with the cars and on motor cycles brought BMW considerable international prestige. This international recognition was well-received in a Germany experiencing a resurgence of national fervour. Racing also speeded product development and BMW's design engineers must have been working flat out at this time with so many different projects in hand. Typical of the recruitment during this period was Dipl Ing Alex von Falkenhausen who was subsequently to be in charge of motor cycle engine design right through to the 1960s. The works teams benefited from the fact that a number of the BMW development engineers were also riders, a precedent set by Rudolf Schleicher back in 1926. In 1934 alone BMW took on 7,500 extra staff and there was plant expansion in Munich and at Eisenach where a new aircraft engine facility was being constructed. It was a fertile period of technical innovation for BMW. Its air-cooled aero-engine was so superior that the Reich Ministry granted the company exclusive production rights. Car production had now advanced to the famous six-cylinder models and the classical kidney grill motif had been created. Bike racing was being changed by the superfast *kompressors* and several technical changes were introduced to the motor cycle world. Frame design switched from pressed steel to tubular steel following improvements in welding technology and the R5, with its hydraulically-damped telescopic front forks, introduced a new era of comfort to the touring biker. Full springing was soon to follow with the arrival of the extremely popular R51. 13,000 of these were to be built before war stopped production and it was a popular export model. It also sold well to the German police and heralded the regular sales which BMW was subsequently to achieve with the world's public authorities. By the close of the '30s the armed forces in Bulgaria, Greece, Holland and Rumania as well as Germany were equipped with BMW motor cycles.

From 1936 Germany was re-arming in earnest and BMW formed a military equipment division at Eisenach to produce field guns and infantry equipment. On the outbreak of hostilities in 1939 the firm phased out motor cycle production for the civilian market and transferred much of the tooling to Eisenach where military versions of the R61, R66 and R71 were continued until 1941. Rural Thuringia was considered less of a strategic target than Munich and it was at Eisenach that the famed R75 military outfits were produced. Additional facilities for manufacturing aeroplane engines were opened in Brandenburg, Berlin, and a foundry was started in Bitschweiler. By 1942 BMW had a workforce of 47,346 engaged in the construction of motor cycles, cars and a powerful air-cooled twin radial aero engine which powered the Focke Wulf 190. This was an exceptionally fast German fighter 'plane with a top speed of 660 mph (1,062 km/h). Between 1941 and 1944 BMW engineers developed and began series production of the 003 jet engine. This was the first mass production of a turbojet engine and made the firm a pace setter for the Jet Age. In 1944 an Arado 234 on test, fitted with two of these engines, reached a record-breaking altitude of nearly 45,000 ft (13,500 m). The pendulum was about to swing again and from such heights BMW was soon to be reduced to a very low point. Outside Germany people remembered BMW for the wonderful racing and record-breaking of the pre-war days or for fine motor cycles and superb sports cars now languishing in garages for want of petrol or spares or because their owners were away at the front. Within Germany BMW faced self-destruction orders aimed at preventing its valuable development and production facilities being over-run by the closing armies of the Allies. One of the most desirable prizes was the top secret test rig for high-altitude engine development.

By the end of the war in 1945 Allied bombing had largely destroyed the firm's plants in and around Berlin and over a third of the Munich facilities were in ruins. The Eisenach complex escaped the destruction by bombing but was over-run by the Red Army forces and was completely lost to BMW. The old Dixi-werke was eventually re-opened in 1946 as the Eisenach Motoren Werke and for ten years produced a pressed-steel version of the pre-war R35 model. This machine, identified after complaints from BMW by its white and red EMW emblem, was sold in the eastern bloc countries until the German Democratic Republic rationalised its motor cycle production at the old DKW factory in Zschopau, southwest of Dresden. The best of the jigs and tooling at Eisenach including the R75 production line was confiscated and shipped back to the USSR. Here they were later to be put to use producing Ural and Dneiper motor cycle combinations.

In Munich itself conflicting orders from the Allied control authorities allowed BMW quickly to resume a limited form of peacetime production. On August 29 1945 the Ordnance Production Control of the 3rd US Army gave permission for the limited production of farm equipment, cooking utensils, bicycle trailers, 21,000 bicycles and even 100 R23 motor cycles. Part of the BMW factories were also being used as a vehicle repair centre for the American Army. Yet on October 1 Major Eugene Keller Jr of the Headquarters Military Government was ordering the Head Mayor of Munich to organise the dismantling of the BMW plants and the crating of all jigs and machine tools for shipment to the USA. This muddle gave heart to the BMW management and a petition was drawn up by Kurt Donath, chief of BMW, seeking to alter these instructions. The appearance of the signature of the irrepressible H.J. Aldington, the head of BMW's British Concessionaire, AFN Ltd, on his petition is a tale in itself and is partly told in Chapter 10. The petition seems to have worked and limited peacetime production continued in what was left of the factory buildings and with the jigs and machine tools which had not been shipped to Detroit, USA, or Bristol, England. It seems clear now that this confiscation did not extend to many of the valuable development plans and prototypes which were to form the basis of the post-war period of reconstruction. It also appears to have been the case that BMW was able safely to secure a number of motor cycle engine blocks which they were later able to use in restarting production. Another survivor of the war and the confused peace was one of the supercharged racers which quickly found itself back in Georg Meier's hands to begin winning races and restoring BMW's badly dented self-image.

For a second time this century heavy war reparations slowed Germany's recovery from destruction and demolition. Again the climb back for the company was based on the motor cycle and in 1948 the Allied Control Commission allowed BMW to resume production of bikes up to 250 cc capacity. It was to be 1953 before the rebuilding of the old Munich works was fully completed, but makeshift production lines now created the R24. This used the pre-war R23 chassis with engine improvements and a four-speed gearbox. A one-off machine was shown at the 1948 Geneva Motor Show at which 50 manufacturers, including 16 British firms, exhibited and the first production machine was raffled amongst the BMW workers.

Sales of motor cycles in Europe at this time were not easy as the market was flooded with war surplus machines. However, petrol shortages and the chaotic state of public transport did help to create a healthy demand. In 1949 BMW managed to produce and sell 9,450 motor cycles, many of them made up from pre-war parts which had survived the bombing. By 1950 12,000 R24 models had left the production lines and its successor, the R25 with rear springing, was available. The same year BMW put the R51/2, the first post-war twin, into series production. It looked like an R51 but its 1938 price of 1,595 RM had become 2,750 DM as the German mark regained some parity with the rest of the world's currencies. Within a year, however, BMW launched a completely new twin, the 252 engine which remained in production for 18 years. The other new model of 1951 was the R67 which appeared later in a special sidecar version able to handle the heavy TR500 touring sidecar. Slowly exports also restarted to Britain and the first bikes crossed the Atlantic to what was to become BMW's major motor cycle export market in the '60s and '70s.

The future of BMW hinged on motor cycle production in the early '50s and by 1953 post-war production had already reached 100,000. In 1952 the buoyancy of motor cycle sales encouraged the unveiling of the R68, the first BMW production bike to have a genuine 100 mph (160 km/h) capability. About a fifth of these big bikes were exported, with many going to the USA. Just as things seemed to be picking up well, the motor cycle market suddenly slumped. BMW saw its peak production of nearly 30,000 machines in 1954 fall to just over 5,000 in 1957. It seemed as if the 1920s' story was being repeated as people began getting off motor cycles and out of combinations and into something better. Too many bike manufacturers were in competition and Germany alone had 26 companies from Adler to Zündapp. Aero engine production had only just been re-started and BMW had not yet sorted out its car production strategy. The generally improving European economy wanted something better than a motor cycle for private transport, but it was a long way from being ready for eight-cylinder luxury vehicles such as the type 502. The stop-gap solution when it arrived was almost as bizarre at the other extreme. BMW purchased a licence from the Italian Iso company and put a motor cycle engine into a low-cost small car called the Isetta. These vehicles were known in English-speaking countries as bubble cars and in Germany as *das rollendei Ei* (the rolling egg). Sales of this little town runabout reached 200,000 and an assembly plant in Brighton, England, was set up. In 1957 the stretched version of the Isetta appeared with four wheels and the R50 engine, but it was unsuccessful as a design. Fortunately, BMW already had its successor, the celebrated 700 coupé, in the pipeline, but as the '50s drew to a close the future for the company looked bleak indeed.

In 1959 the annual report showed the firm to be in the red. Plans were discussed to merge with arch rivals Daimler-Benze AG and even the old-established Glas company was asked to consider a takeover. The motor cycle side of the business looked destined to become part of the Zweirad Union of Nuremberg which had already swallowed the old DKW, Hercules and Victoria banners. The Allach aero-engine facilities were sold off to the German commercial vehicle manufacturer, MAN Turbo GmbH. For a while shareholders, bankers and accountants held BMW in their hands but eventually it was decided to carry on. A management shake up brought in new methods and policies and a more vigorous promotional and marketing strategy was adopted. It was to be the turn of the motor car to spearhead the company's move back into profit.

During the 1960s first the 700 series and then models 1500, 1600 and 1800 poured from the Munich production lines as the bike output fell to an all-time low of 4,700 units (1969). In contrast to the glamorous image of the cars, BMW motor cycles had become over-engineered and too expensive. In the face of the newly-emerging superbike image they looked heavy and old-fashioned. The new style motor cycles had been launched by Honda with its CB750-4, quickly developed by the rest of the Japanese industry and was influencing the big bike expansion in the Italian factories of Benelli, Ducati, Laverda and Moto Guzzi. By 1969 even the old favourite quarter-litre model, the saviour of BMW on several occasions, fell victim to falling sales. The R27, last of a long line of BMW singles now sadly found itself too staid, too expensive and too exclusive to survive the torrent of small, fashionable machines which were flooding Europe and the USA from Japan. For a while it looked as if the only possibility was for BMW to withdraw completely from motor cycle production.

In 1969 all bike production for BMW was banished to West Berlin close to the historical Juliusturm in the Spandau district. Berlin, capital of Germany and its largest industrial and commercial city before the Second World War, had a BMW presence during the 1930s. Now, in the peculiar circumstances of post-war reconstruction, the attractions of West Berlin were more to do with national pride and Federal government taxation inducements than tradition. In German law Berlin is a state *(Land)* of the Federal Republic of Germany but, under the terms of the Quadripartite Agreement between the Great

From the sublime to the ridiculous? BMW's car range in the mid-'50s, the BMW 500 and the 502 outside 76 Lerchenauerstrasse, Munich (AFN Ltd—the W.H. Aldington collection).

Powers which is the supreme authority, Berlin is not a constituent part of the Federal Republic. The effect is to make West Berlin a special case and considerable financial incentives for both employer and employee exist to promote the industrial development of the isolated city. Another consequence of Berlin's position is an aging population and the employment of many *Gastarbeiten* (foreign 'guest workers'). Freight can pass along access corridors to West Germany in sealed vehicles, but it is not a particularly efficient system over the long distances to the south.

The heart of the company continues to expand in Bavaria, its traditional base. In 1963 shareholders received their first dividend for 20 years and in the period 1960-4 BMW ploughed 136 million DM back into the business to finance the enormously popular 'New Range' of cars. The company workforce doubled to 12,000 and in 1966 BMW took over Glas GmbH of Dingolfing, now reduced to manufacturing the Goggo bubble car. BMW was now more than ever identified with what sociologists have called the 'strainers', the aspiring service class. As they prospered in the 'Swinging '60s' so did BMW. In 1968 new car production facilities and a central spares depot were started at Dingolfing, 60 miles (96 km) north-east of Munich. Annual car production was now running at 145,000 vehicles. Halfway between Dingolfing and Munich another plant at Landshut produces BMW parts including drive shafts, steering columns and various plastic items.

At the start of the '70s it could be said that BMW had regained its place as one of the world's most prestigious motor vehicle manufacturers. 23,000 employees produced 166,000 cars and nearly 19,000 motor cycles with a turnover of 1,900 million DM. As if to endorse its world ranking, 1972 saw the opening of its 325 ft (100 m) high, 21 storey, all-aluminium headquarters tower. This audacious design of four huge cylinders cantilevered from a central spine was the work of the Viennese architect Karl Schwanzer. It forms a three-dimensional replica of the famous BMW logo and that is also reproduced in the unusual concrete bowl at the foot of the tower which houses the company museum. The headquarters houses 2,000 administrative staff in open plan offices filled with potted plants and room dividers. High speed lifts rush from the directors' suite at the top to the basement garages to keep pace with the frantic activity of the building. Opposite sprawls the high technology factory where BMW cars are made. From the higher

Above Der Grösster Vierzylinder der Welt, *BMW AG head office in Munich. The concrete bowl houses the famous BMW museum. The entrance to the car plant is to the left* (BMW).

Below *BMW's test track at Ascheim* (BMW).

offices there are amazing views of Munich itself showing how much the city has expanded since those early days when the firm was part of the outskirts. Completion of its headquarters building in 1972 allowed BMW, already Munich's number one manufacturing employer, to put its best face forward when the world visited the city for the XX Olympiad. It was from this silver and blue eyrie that BMW executives planned and implemented the overseas expansion which was to change the Bavarian Motor Works into a multi-national company of international dimensions.

Research and development have always been key posts at BMW. The company has a consistent record of putting profits back into development work and has been fortunate with many of its design engineers who have been prepared to leave the drawing board to test their ideas on road or track. In the early days designers such as Schleicher and von Falkenhausen tested on the old Munich airfield adjoining the factory but, since 1971, BMW has used its own advanced technology proving grounds at Ascheim, just north of Munich. Here cars and motor cycles designed and developed in the research and development division can be put through the most gruelling proving programme possible while under total electronic surveillance. Facilities include a high-speed road track, a variety of off-road surfaces and an elaborate wind tunnel. This has played an important part in designing motor cycle fairings to achieve the best possible aerodynamic performance. Always a fiercely independent company, BMW continues to invest heavily in its future and, for its size, more than matches the research and development effort of the major Japanese manufacturers.

BMW had got back into profitability by creating the right formula for its cars, now it was able to breath fresh life into the motor cycles. The Stroke series enabled the company to create a new, exclusive image aimed at the rapidly growing leisure market of the '70s. The new models featured the best of the BMW concept with a luxury specification which was able to carve an exclusive niche in the motor cycle market safe from the mass-production manufacturers and their enormous model mix.

Some BMW buffs would dispute this description of events, claiming that the company effectively stopped making motor cycles when the classic R69S was phased out. The majority of BMW bikers would, however, be puzzled by such a view because most of those who now ride BMWs have only done so over the past decade. Between 1970 and 1980 the company doubled annual car production while bike sales rose from 12,000 units to 29,000 units. The peak year was 1977 when motor cycle production in Berlin hit 31,000, just about the maximum output for the factory. In this ten-year period BMW produced 264,760 machines and enjoyed record levels of sales in the USA, France, Britain and Italy, as well as Germany itself. This outpouring of motor cycles probably accounts for about half of the total of BMWs guessed to be still running on the roads of the world. The marketing people would claim that such a volume of sales speaks for itself; the bikes would not sell this way unless the public was convinced that they were good value and probably the best all round motor cycle design available.

BMW motor cycles: production and sales

	Motor cycle production	*Motor cycle sales*
1970	12,287	12,346
1971	18,772	18,898
1972	21,122	21,045
1973	20,856	19,918
1974	23,160	25,189
1975	25,566	25,553
1976	28,209	28,171
1977	31,515	31,231
1978	29,580	26,592
1979	24,415	27,339
1980	29,260	29,263

This growth was pleasing to the shareholders, chiefly the Quandt family, and justified the faith which had kept the two-wheel side of the business going through the 1959 financial crisis. This exciting period in the firm's development has meant considerable expansion of the payroll and the addition of many new facilities in the wider world of the company. Over 37,000 employees work directly for BMW and there are thousands more around the world associated with the company in subsidiaries, concessions and dealerships. Currently at the top is Dipl Ing Eberhard von Kuenheim who has been managing director since 1970. He heads a small executive group of seven directors who run the company for the 20 board members and the shareholders. This small management team is typical of the BMW organisation and has been developed to speed communication and keep the decision makers in direct touch with the business. The company structure shows just how complex a combine BMW is, with extensive interests both at home and abroad. As the company expanded there has been considerable experimentation with the organisation to maintain the momentum of responsibility. At the time of writing the parent company is BMW AG in Munich. Since 1976 the motor cycle business has been run as a separate division a short distance east of the main Munich complex. BMW Motorrad GmbH is responsible for sales, parts and service and marketing. In 1981 the production facilities and the research and development section reverted to the control of the main company. Currently heading BMW Motorrad is Herr Gerlinger with Dr Aurich managing the Berlin production facilities.

Newcomers to BMW have considerable pride and satisfaction in the excellent working conditions the company provides for its employees. The factory workers are bussed in on each shift, there are subsidised canteen arrangements, health services, nurseries for young children and extensive social and sports facilities. Apart from the old Berlin factory most of the accommodation both in Germany and abroad is stylish and modern and very much in keeping with the company's exclusive image. The rewards working for BMW include above average levels of pay, substantial holiday bonuses and worthwhile benefits such as a cheap car purchase plan. Fringe benefits, including cars, are fixed by rank in the hierarchy and the system works world-wide to include the subsidiaries.

Although these daughter companies mostly hire their own staff, BMW is structured on an international basis and promotion can be made between countries. Recently, for example, Jean Pierre Bailby moved from BMW France to head the motor cycle group for BMW of North America Inc. Many of the staff are young and well-qualified technically. The company practice of creating small task teams with short links in the decision-making chain does mean, however, that exceptional dedication to the job is expected. If a task requires it key employees can find themselves working long hours each week at a high level of pressure.

The size of the company alone makes it somewhat bureaucratic and a good deal of paper work is generated by the fine detail which the management considers worth reporting and recording. The task is eased by the sophistication of the data processing equipment which is now widely used. Some idea of the energy generated can be gained by standing outside the Munich headquarters and watching the company at work. On one side the car factory hums with high technology output. In the streets lorries come and go with car bodies and parts and every so often fleets of buses arrive and depart with employees from outlying districts. From the enormous underground car parks emerge a constant stream of BMW cars pursuing this or that company business while inside the tower the lift-coming bells play a constant tune as staff are shuttled between the 21 floors.

The tightly knit management structure of BMW in Germany has been used as a model for the major overseas subsidiaries. It allows the business to be run very efficiently using a limited number of heads backed up by telex and computer links and the occasional face to face meeting. Under such pressure the teamwork does not allow much surplus to be carried within the organisation. Now management responsibilities can change very rapidly compared with the times of the old guard such as Friz, Schleicher and Popp, who served long apprenticeships. A number of heads have moved in the internal management shake-ups of the 1970s and in connection with the taking over of many of the concessionaires. The single-mindedness of this exercise has inevitably ruffled feelings and not everyone has been convinced that such drastic action was necessary. It has also meant that some of the important decision makers within BMW are new to motor cycles and have had little opportunity so far to play themselves into the biking side of the business. Results have, however, convinced BMW that they can market their products more effectively using their own organisation rather than using an independent importer. Clear lines of responsibility and standardised procedures might remove some of the colour from the business, but it does lead to more orderly production and marketing. Longer term planning becomes possible and the closer links to the parent company make operations more flexible, such as switching the model mix around to where the market demand is strongest.

So in a deliberate way BMW has elected to go for centralised control of its fortunes. The obvious risk is that, if important decision-making becomes too remote and exclusive, the market needs could be misjudged. In the fiercely competitive motor cycle market today, a company with such a small range of models can hardly afford to carry any flops. For every motor cycle BMW makes it is now producing some 12 cars and they are obviously the present pre-occupation of the company. Indeed, the visitor to BMW in Munich will look hard to locate where the action is for motor cycles. Some critics, comparing earlier golden times, complain that company policy is too heavily oriented to the

50 years of BMW cars. From left to right the 15 bhp Dixi (1928), the 30 bhp 303 (1933), the 50 bhp 326 (1936), the 95 bhp V8 502 (1954), the 90 bhp 1802 (1968) and the 197 bhp 733i (1980). This progressive development is the basis of the company's present fortunes (BMW).

needs of the car side of the business and the motor cycles have become the poor cousins. Yet it must be acknowledged that within the motor cycle division staff clearly insist that BMW continues the manufacture of bikes for the return and not the tradition. Maybe sentiment saved the bikes during the motor cycle slump of the '60s, but since then they have earned their way. Considerable expansion of the bike production facilities is planned to take place over the next few years and development work on new engines and frames will soon add another chapter to the continuing saga of the Max Friz concept.

The BMW family in Germany

Head Office: Bayerische Motoren Werke AG, Munich. 500 million DM (nominal capital 1980). **Motor cycle marketing:** BMW Motorrad GmbH, Munich. 12 million DM. **Marine engine sales:** BMW Marine GmbH, Munich. 6 million DM. **Leasing of cars and motor cycles:** BMW Leasing GmbH, Munich. 10 million DM. **Finance company:** BMW Kredit Bank GmbH, Frankfurt. 13.5 million DM. **Motorsport products:** BMW Motorsport GmbH, Munich. 0.02 million DM. **Retail sales:** Schorsch Meier GmbH, Munich. 0.30 million DM. **Parts manufacture:** Fahrzeug und Maschinenfabrik GmbH, Landshut. 0.30 million DM. **Motor cycle assembly:** BMW Maschinenfabrik Spandau GmbH, Berlin. 6 million DM. **Property company:** BMW Grundstucksgesellschaft GmbH, Berlin. 0.02 million DM. **Insurance services:** Bavaria Wirtschafts-agentur GmbH, Munich. 0.2 million DM. **Tourist agency (51% ownership):** Bavaria-Lloyd Reiseburo GmbH, Munich. 0.02 million DM.

The BMW family around the world

Holding companies: BMW Holding AG, Zurich, Switzerland. 10 million Fr. BMW(US) Holding Corp, Wilmington, Del, USA. $8 million. **Importing companies:** BMW Austria GmbH. Salzburg, Austria. 45 million Sch. BMW Belgium SA/NV, Kontich, Belgium. 66 million Fr. BMW (Schweiz) AG, Dielsdorf, Switzerland. 0.5 million Fr. BMW France SA, Bois d'Arcy, France. 16.5 million Fr. BMW of North America Inc, Montvale, NJ, USA. $4 million. BMW(GB) Ltd, Bracknell, England. £4 million. BMW Italia SpA, Milan, Italy. 3 million Lir. BMW Australia Ltd, Melbourne, Australia. $0.5 million Aus. Nederland BV, 's-Gravenhage, The Netherlands. 0.5 million Gld. Balcom Trading Company Inc, (BMW Japan), Tokyo, Japan. $0.03 million. BMW Distributors Eastern Canada Ltd, Scarborough, Ont, Canada. $0.02 million. **Finance company:** BMW Overseas Enterprises NV, Willemstad, Curaçao, NA. 2 million DM. **Production and importing company:** BMW (South Africa) Pty Ltd, Pretoria, South Africa. 12.9 million Rd. **Leasing of cars, bikes and boats:** BMW Italia Leasing SpA, Palazzolo di Sona, Italy. 3 million Lir. **Development and production of light diesel engines (co-ownership):** BMW-Steyr Motoren GmbH, Steyr, Austria. 800 million Sch.

8

Making the ultimate riding machine

A BMW motor cycle consists of between 4,000 and 5,000 single parts. Each one is the result of deliberate selection, persistent development and careful manufacture under the strictest quality control. BMW feel that only the very best is good enough for the ultimate riding machines. The transformation from bits to bike takes place in the factory at Spandau in Berlin.

At first sight BMW Motorrad GmbH looks like any of the factory complexes which line the wide roads of the Spandau district of West Berlin. It occupies a length of the Juliusturm which, in the spring of 1981, was a muddy construction site where the Berlin U-Bahn was being expanded. The factory is low red-brick and scattered in a number of buildings and outhouses. It has the solid functionalism of 19th century construction with little of the fancy gloss of modern times. It is no surprise to learn that it was once an arms and gunpowder factory belonging to the Prussian government of the Second Reich. In 1928 it was acquired by Siemens Halske AG and used to produce aeroplane engines and rotary hoes. It passed to BMW in 1939 when the company needed additional space for the construction of its Ju 52 aero engines. By 1940 production was fully stretched and the plant employed 10,000 workers.

Five years later much of Berlin was in ruins. The plant escaped serious damage from bombing but it did not escape the losses from war reparations. In what was eventually left of the dismantled factory a token force of 100 began making farm tools and repairing motor cars. At the time of the Berlin Airlift, in 1948, the plant was producing machine tools and a year later began to produce motor cycle parts for the main assembly lines in Munich. By 1958 the engines and gearboxes of the R50S and R69S were being made in Berlin as the company as a whole struggled for survival. In the rationalisation which followed the 1959/60 crisis the decision was taken to switch all motor cycle assembly to the Spandau factory, although transmissions would continue to be made in the south. The first 'Berliner' model was the Stroke 5 series and 400 workers turned out 30 of them a day. By 1975 the 100,000th motor cycle had left the Berlin assembly line and the 1,300 workers drew lots for it. Daily production was now up to 120 and the whole motor cycle was being produced in Berlin. Bike production became completely independent in 1976 with the creation of the separate division, BMW Motorrad GmbH.

The boom in sales at this time put considerable pressure on the Berlin work facilities and frame welding had to be moved into nearby rented workshops to make room for the new, compact R45/65 models. New workshop accommodation became available on site in 1979, but it was used for the production of brake discs and exhaust manifolds for cars. The car plants in southern Germany were also finding production space a problem at a time of expanding demand. By 1981 motor cycle production of between 135 and 145 units a day was stretching the Berlin factory capacity to its maximum. Particular pressure is felt in the paint shops and the final assembly. It is now planned to open new assembly facilities which will enable production targets to be raised from 33,000 a year to 60,000. The numbers of employees at Spandau is expected to rise to 1,800 by 1983. About 60 per cent of the skilled work-force are of Yugoslav and Turkish origins and the 456 assembly workers are deployed in seven sections. 76 work on frame building, 38 build the engines, 15 are in the paint shop, 38 deal with galvanising, 135 assemble the bikes and a similar number are employed in the finishing area, while 19 pack machines for shipping.

Some 40 per cent of a BMW bike is made completely by BMW in Berlin. This includes the engine, the frame and the gearbox. Other parts such as the electrics, suspension units, seats, wheels and brakes are bought in from contractors under very strict quality control inspection. Some of this quality control is carried out by BMW staff actually in the factories where the parts are being manufactured. The instruments and most of the running gear come from German factories with the brakes and alloy wheels being made in Italy. The tyres most commonly found on BMW bikes are made by the Munich-based Metzeler firm or Continental in Hannover. Recently, type approval has also been granted to the French Michelin company and to American-developed Dunlop tyres made in Japan. Final assembly is very much a hand-crafted business with frequent

Stroke 6 BMWs being assembled at the Berlin factory (BMW).

inspections to check accuracy and performance. A fifth of the workforce are in quality control jobs and, to further improve efficiency, BMW is attempting to train all assembly workers to take responsibility for their own inspection checks.

Munich and the marketing divisions of the importing companies estimate their model mix requirements one year ahead and Berlin plans its production accordingly. The exact orders from the dealers are consolidated three months ahead and colour requirements are confirmed four weeks in advance. A development recently has been to identify the model by its colour, although the North American market still demands brighter colours than Europe. For many years a BMW buyer could have any colour so long as it was black and, in many eyes, it still remains the classic colour. The range includes the compacts, the dual-purpose bike, the 1-litre machines and those for public authority use and they can pass along the assembly line in any order or combination. In 1980 the assembly line brought forth 47 per cent of the big bikes, 40 per cent R45/65, 9 per cent public authority machines and 4 per cent of the new R80 G/S dual purpose models. Now that BMW has more control over the major importing companies, production planning can be more accurately based on development programmes and agreed target sales. The competition amongst the world's manufacturers has made 'moving metal' a top priority and investment plans require each subsidiary to substantially increase its total sales. The current car boom means that every BMW car leaving the factory is already forward sold, but that is certainly not going to be the case in the future with motor cycles.

The power plant, the heart of a BMW bike, starts life in the mechanical production part of the factory. Here numerically-controlled drilling and milling machines convert the rough aluminium block castings into the polished and functional engine block. Alongside crankshafts, camshafts, connecting rods, flywheels, drive shaft housing and brake discs are being heat-treated, turned, drilled, polished and balanced ready for engine assembly. Some idea of the complexity of these operations can be judged by following the progress of an RT crankshaft which in the transformation from rough casting to the balanced article loses 1½ kg of metal. The famous engines take shape under skilled and practised hands on a short, oval assembly line. In a series of well-drilled movements, accompanied by the frenetic clatter of power tools, the empty engine casing is filled carefully like a chocolate box with a balanced crankshaft, camshaft, oil pump, flywheel, gear train, clutch assembly, oil sump, connecting rods, pistons and barrels and overhead valve gear. Next, already-assembled ignition units, starter motor, alternator, air filter and carburettors are attached. Finally the plugs are fitted and every three minutes a shiny finished engine swings off the line in search of a frame. An engine is selected at random for bench testing as part of the inspection process.

Part of the explanation of the bikes' excellent roadholding and handling can be found in the nature of their frame technology. BMW has had long experience of frame development, much of it race-proved, and the company is justly proud that it has always used advanced manufacturing techniques able to complement the design of the bike. The modern bikes use a closed double loop frame which has been gas-welded from special lightweight steel tube. At stress points the tubes are of oval-drawn section and the backbone tube of the frame is double-skinned for strength. Neat welding seams and careful attention to corrosion proofing ensure a long life of service. Remotely-controlled robot welders create the frames and the finished article is checked for accuracy using an optical alignment jig. Since 1969 BMW frames have been too flexible for sidecar use and today's design has been based on solo touring requirements. Riders seriously interested in pushing standard bikes to the limits are tempted to strengthen their frames with extra bracing developed by high performance specialists such as San Jose Racing in the USA. However, dealer sponsors such as Vincent Davey of Gus Kuhn, who raced Stroke 5 machines, claim that the standard frame is more than adequate for the job.

The parts for the BMW motor cycle finally come together in the assembly shop which is on the middle floor of a three-storey building. Here a remarkably short, slow-moving and U-shaped line carries up to 15 bikes in various stages of creation. The first operation involves bolting the engine to the frame and then the seat is fitted. At the next station the swinging arm and the front exhaust pipes are put into place, with the rear brake assembly and drive shaft rapidly following. At the bottom of the U-turn the wiring is clipped into place, the ignition key taped to the seat and the rear shockers are attached. Returning up the line, first the forks and front wheel are swung into place then the headlight assembly and pannier frame are fitted. The handlebars and control cables follow with the mudguards, rear wheel and silencers completing the finished bike. At the final station the bikes' brakes are bled and a close inspection is made before the machines descend by lift to the final assembly area on the ground floor.

Above the assembly line is a paint shop where frames are dip painted after electro-static undercoating and then passed through a drying area. In one of the most traditional operations of the whole manufacturing process, petrol tanks have their coach lines painted by hand in just a couple of flowing movements. The completed tanks are then despatched to the ground floor where the final assembly operations take place. Here 250 items on each bike are checked and tanks and fairings are fitted. At first each bike is fitted with a battered dummy tank while the final checks take place. The bike is fired up for the first time, carburation and timing adjustments are made and then it is ridden on to a rolling road.

This is the most active part of the factory. Space is very limited and the rows of shiny new bikes contrast with the rather shabby interior of this old factory. The familiar noise of the BMW twin fills the air as bikes are started and the testers weave in and out of the tiny boxed rolling road area. Just outside this building a dozen or so motor cycles are standing with their engines ticking over on

A BMW frame takes its correct shape (BMW).

The rolling road at BMW Motorrad, Berlin (BMW).

longer term tests. To one side there is a special test rig for checking the CO_2 emissions on bikes destined for the USA. Through the glass windows of the rolling road area the test riders can be seen putting each bike through a rigorous one-minute testing procedure. Engine speed, acceleration, gear change, braking, steering, suspension and lighting are all checked and the tester is sensitive enough to be able to feel that the wheels are running true and that there are no unusual mechanical noises being made. Time up, the road stops, the swing doors open and tester and machine shoot out into the final rectification area where any faults can be put right. In fact, defects are rather rare at this stage because of the high standard of precision used in the manufacture of component parts and the quality of the assembly inspections. The use of fine tolerances and careful balancing of engine parts mean that BMW motors normally run true and strong from the first firing.

At last the ugly duckling becomes a swan as the old test tank is replaced by a gleaming new one. The bike now moves into the packing area where it is sprayed with anti-corrosion liquid and the front forks are protected with plastic sheeting. The last act is to settle the machine in its wooden transport container, heat-shrink heavy gauge plastic film around the box and stencil on its destination. 30 of these crates will fit on to one container lorry and three out of four of them will be destined for Hamburg, the docks and overseas. At the time of the author's visit the loading bay was crowded with crates holding RTs for Italy, 80 G/Ss for Austria, R45s for Denmark, a CS for Britain and police bikes for Mexico. Made in Berlin to be ridden across the world!

Production methods at Spandau are very labour intensive and rather antiquated by modern standards of motor cycle manufacture. Visiting BMW Berlin in 1981 was in many ways like going back to part of BSA's Small Heath plant a decade earlier. A gentle and leisurely production operation based on traditional craft skills and high quality raw materials. Little of a BMW motor cycle is made at the frontiers of technology, although much of it results from tried and tested craftsmanship and skill. When the new extension to the motor cycle plant is in operation it will feature the latest and most advanced production equipment comparable to that used in the Munich car factories. For the moment, however, output is handicapped by plant limitations. BMW's handcrafted production looks minute set against the statistics of the Japanese motor cycle industry. In 1980 Japan's bike manufacturers produced nearly 6.5 million bikes of which just over half were exported. By comparison West Germany produced under 300,000 of which barely a tenth were over 50 cc machines. BMW is West Germany's only manufacturer of big bikes and in 1980 it produced 29,260 machines. At the top end of the market this did, however, yield a turnover of 185 million DM.

Since production switched to Spandau this relatively small production unit has turned out over 300,000 motor cycles. During the period 1970-80 production more than doubled and the range included 13 different models.

Motor cycle production 1970-80

R50	7,466
R60	46,747
R75	61,676
R90	21,105
R90S	17,464
R100/7/T	18,826
R100S	12,393
R100RS	21,557
R80/7	14,038
R100RT	10,080
R45	17,488
R65	14,254
R80 G/S	1,666
Total	*264,760*

Comparison of sales in two countries show how local market conditions can alter the model mix demand. The figures for West Germany are actual 1980 registrations and those for Britain are 1981 target sales.

Packing an RS for travel overseas (BMW).

Model mix demand

	R45	R65	R80 G/S	R100	R100 CS	R100 RT	R100 RS
West Germany	42%	18%	9%	6%	8%	8%	9%
United Kingdom	5%	20%	9%	18%	7%	19%	22%

Similarly the export percentages by model show which motor cycles are most popular on the home market.

Exports by model

R45	R65	R80G/S	R100	R100CS	R100RT	R100RS
18%	71%	65%	86%	51%	80%	73%

In 1980 BMW Motorrad earned 185 million DM from the sale of motor cycles, 74 million DM from parts and 6 million DM from accessories. This 265 million DM represents less than 4 per cent of the total company turnover. Such accounts make it very plain that the BMW of the '80s is primarily in the motor car business.

One difficulty BMW faces in expanding its motor cycle production is to persuade the world that it will not mean any lowering of its exclusive, hand-crafted quality. Indeed, owners already complain that the quality image is being oversold and that in reality standards are not what they were. Any greater expansion of output might lead to cutting corners and a further compromise in quality. Traditionalists tend to be suspicious of the glossy advertising and see it as being pre-occupied with cosmetic rather than genuine improvements. Each new model gets closely scrutinised to see where the cost accountants are saving on the specification compared with previous machines. A common complaint is that the quality of chromium plating and paintwork is of a lower standard. But such comparisons are difficult to sustain as new developments bring in new materials and different production techniques. Many of the chromed parts are now in stainless steel or in bump- and corrosion-proof plastics. Moreover, it can be shown that the BMW specification for chrome and paint work still exceeds the standards set by the German TUV type approval requirements. The Technische Uberwachung Verein is Germany's strict technical inspection and control association which checks all vehicle specifications and modifications before granting type approval for use on the nation's roads. Purists may object, of course, to plastic on principle, but the efficiency of the material can hardly be disputed.

Sometimes the criticisms can be explained by styling considerations rather than a lowering of standards. Thus the hard seats of the RTs resulted from finding space for the fashionable rear fairing. Design practice favours shorty mudguards, although most riders see greater advantages in the deep guards now only normally available on public authority machines. For the R65LS BMW stylists have created what they call the 'flyline', a sporty look which links the front mudguard to the cockpit with its integrated spoiler

The R69S, the most aristocratic of thoroughbreds.

The 1981 R100RS. Performance: over 124 mph (200 km/h) and will accelerate from 0 to 100 km/h in 4.6 seconds (BMW).

then through the tank and seat to the rear-end tail in one smooth line.

In some instances suspicion about a modification may be based on traditional experience and technical proof can eventually demonstrate the advantages of the change. Thus some reservations have been expressed about the new linerless aluminium cylinder barrels which have been spray-coated to increase engine life, improve heat dissipation and lower oil consumption. Losing the possibility to re-bore becomes less of a loss when it can be shown that Galnikal cylinders are likely to outlive both rider and machine. Indeed, their strength has already resulted in BMW extending the running in period for the linerless engines suggesting that they must be tougher than the old cast linings. Nor is this technology radically new or untested. Outboard engines for boats have used this system for years and, back in the 1950s, the Italian Iso company developed a coated cylinder lining for its little 236 cc Isetta bubble car.

Another object of controversy is the blueing of exhaust pipes. The front bend in the silencers of most BMW bikes will be seen to be a straw/blue colour and this permanent change occurs within the first few miles of the bike's ridden life. There are buffs who claim that it is possible to ride so carefully that this blueing will not occur, but the exhaust design makes it almost inevitable. The power needs, fuel consumption and noise level requirements of a BMW motor cycle demand as narrow an exhaust pipe as possible. The flat twin layout requires there to be a sharp bend to the exhaust pipe where it exits the cylinder block and hence there is a localised hot spot. Fitting double-skinned exhausts, as on many Japanese bikes, would prevent discolouring, but it would also restrict heat dissipation from the engine and disturb the optimum working temperature of the boxer design. Criticism does not come from all BMW owners because some cussedly like their blued exhausts, seeing them as a witness to how fast they ride! Since 1981 several models have come fitted with matt black exhaust systems and for these this particular issue does not even arise.

Sometimes a complaint arises about standards because an individual rider has special uses in

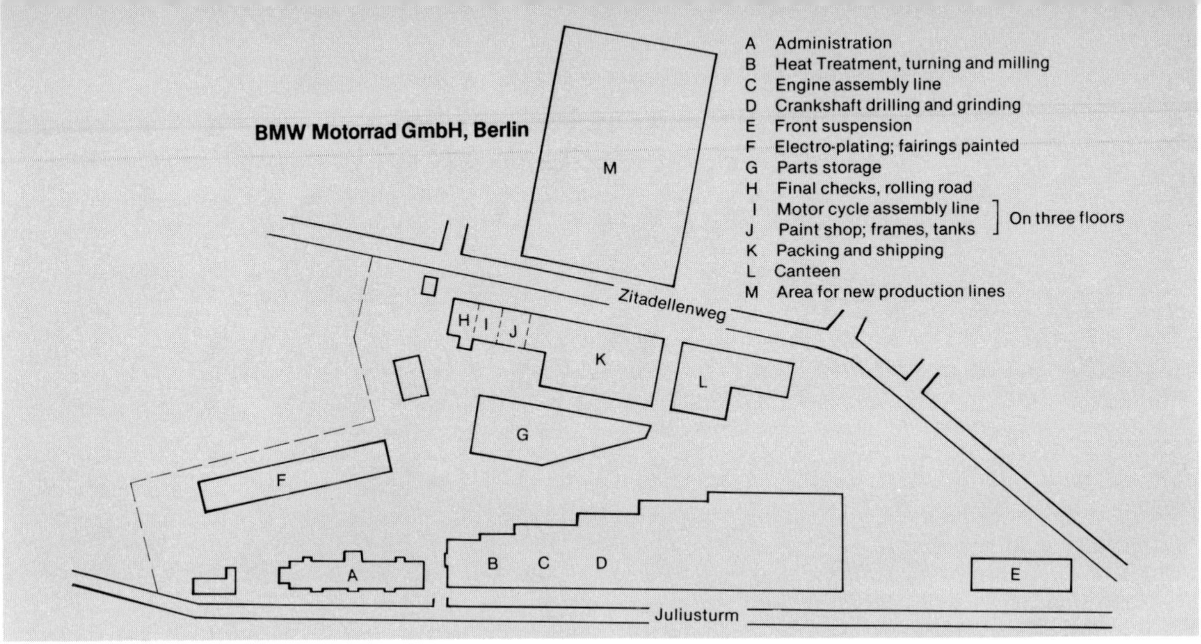

mind. Thus chair addicts will rue the fact that since 1969 BMW frames have not been strong enough to accept sidecar fittings. The present frame is too light, the front fork travel is too great and the front fork castor or trail is too positive for sidecar use. The commuters in a cold and wet climate are more likely to find their BMW rusting from frequent applications of winter salt than the fair weather brigade who lay their machines up for the winter months. Equally BMW must pay a price for selling in a limited but discriminating market. The owners are uncommonly articulate and the fact that any mechanical device will occasionally play rogue gets lost when it involves a new, expensive BMW motor cycle. If you think you are buying the best then human nature demands nothing less than the best. Failures due possibly to inept servicing or poor riding technique grow in the mind to shoddy workmanship and the complaint of falling standards. The fact that BMW as a manufacturer, maintains a generous warranty service means that the slightest doubt in an owner's mind can lead to a claim which fuels the statistics on declining standards.

It may serve to illustrate this dilemma about standards to compare what was claimed and what analysts of the time said about two of BMW's classic models. The 1969 R69S and the 1976 R100RS make an interesting contrast between the old and the new. The reader will come to a personal opinion, but probably most owners would agree that today's models are better riding machines. BMW itself would probably settle for that, satisfied that the company tradition of developing and improving the marque was being fulfilled.

Trend setters may still feel that the pace of change is too slow and accuse BMW of being old-fashioned and conservative. They charge the company with dragging its feet on new models with alternative engine formats, anti-dive suspension, fuel injection and the other biking innovations of the '80s. Some angry critics even accuse the company of arrogance in describing its apparent reluctance to react to criticisms of gearboxes, oil seal failure, inadequate electrics, rapid tyre wear and weak propstands. The virtue BMW see in slow, step by step change is seen as evidence that the factory is too remote, over-reliant on tradition and too self-satisfied that it has got the concept right. In defence, BMW can justifiably claim to have maintained an impetus of innovation in motor cycle design over a period of 60-odd years.

Styling exercises such as the Futuro study and the development work known to be well-advanced on the K589 project show that even tradition is not an infallible doctrine. The 1981 models answered a lot of the criticisms and introduced several new-look machines. In the final analysis it must also be remembered that the firm is after all a small-scale motor cycle operation. With such a low level of production it can hardly afford to experiment with limited life models which require expensive re-tooling and costly research and development investment. The giant Japanese concerns can use the economies of scale to adapt to market forces and rapid changes in fashion. BMW is more likely to keep its supporters by continuing to aim at the discerning few and ensuring that its priorities remain safe handling, reliability, comfort and convenience.

9

BMW world-wide

In many ways BMW is as German as sauerkraut and frankfurter sausages. To the rest of the world the company can be identified with the traditional Teutonic values of good workmanship and efficiency, but its origins in the south, in Bavaria, add to the picture a measure of the good life. The products are seen as admirable but also desirable. They command respect yet they can also win love and admiration. Because of the quality of the product BMW has come to be represented in over 130 countries of the world.

Wherever import laws and regulations permit it, a BMW motor cycle can be obtained. Although it is still true to say that BMW vehicles remain rather rare on the world's roads, there are now 2 million cars and approaching ½ a million motor cycles in circulation bearing the white and blue logo. To give the high level of service which BMW owners expect, a network of official dealers has been created that across the world now numbers over 5,000. Over 43,000 employees are part of this international organisation. The BMW network is densest in the 18 countries of Europe where there are over 1,100 motor cycle dealers and some three times that number handling cars only.

Until the late 1960s BMW overseas was handled entirely through official concessionaires and agencies. This meant that the BMW image was maintained by influence and the quality of the exported products. This arrangement can only succeed where there is a good working relationship between the importer and the company and agreement on policies and priorities. Although the importer may know the local market conditions the commitment to the manufacturer is a limited one. If communications are remote and times become difficult the company and the concession may find it impossible to remain in agreement. Certainly during the post-war recovery period BMW's overseas image-building programme was held back because importers lacked confidence in the company's products and its marketing strategies. In Britain during the '60s, for example, the BMW franchise changed hands five times

BMW's Spanish concession, the Madrid head office and main dealers on Avenida Pio XII. The starting place of the 1980 Rideaway for British dealers (BMW).

The stylish head offices of three of BMW's importing companies—Austria, Great Britain and France (BMW).

before the right sort of relationship between the company and its concessionaire could be established.

The real break-through came in the 1970s when the bike boom, buoyed by a boom in car sales, enabled BMW to seize the initiative in many of its overseas markets. Through the '70s the company gradually took over the concessions in its major markets and converted them to wholly-owned subsidiaries. In each case there was a considerable management shake up and extensive investment, often in the form of new administrative and warehousing facilities. Today each 'daughter company' retains a degree of independent action and flexibility to react to local market conditions, but the hand of Munich, managing the needs of the company as a whole, is evident world-wide. The organisation needed for this sort of control is now a lot easier because modern communication systems have shrunk the globe and put every corner of the BMW empire at the end of a telex line or computer link. It is all a far cry from the days when a dealer took an order, posted it to the concessionaires and the customer waited patiently for the bike eventually to appear from far-off Germany.

The story of how BMW's world-wide reputation developed has already been told. In the early days it was the aero engines which won much of the company's international recognition. These engines played a significant part in early aviation history and BMW's pioneering achievements brought not only fame but numerous commercial contracts with overseas airlines. The Ju 52 transport plane, for example, was flown on BMW engines by 30 of the world's airlines. These international contracts also led to development collaboration and early on BMW had technical links with the American Pratt & Whitney company. An unlikely outcome of this arrangement was a prototype 350 cc motor cycle which featured a cylinder head design similar to that used on the Pratt & Whitney Hornet aeroplane engine. Later Karl Popp, the sacked head of BMW, was to cite these trans-Atlantic contacts during his interrogation by the US military at the end of the war. The brilliant track and record successes of the motor cycles and the cars were a stimulus to exports, although strong domestic industries before the Second World War did make the imported BMW something of an exclusive commodity. This international acclaim reached its first peak unfortunately just before hostilities interrupted free world trade. It is only recently that BMW has risen from the national league to become one of the superstars of the world's vehicle manufacturers.

At BMW world motor cycle strategy is decided by the planners in Munich. The resources of the main company are close by to provide assistance and ensure the delivery of the right model range at the right time. Each overseas subsidiary supplies Munich with regular updates on sales and other market intelligence so that production at Berlin and the overall development programme can be accurately matched to world needs. In most countries demand for motor cycles peaks around the same time in the early summer, although, of course, in Australia, South Africa and South America the reversed seasons shift the main sales effort to the opposite time of the year. In some parts of the world such as the American West Coast the kind climate results in a very stable level of demand. Two-thirds of BMW motor cycle sales are made overseas and export orders are shipped direct from the factory through Hamburg.

BMW Motorrad also co-ordinates orders for parts and technical accessories which are freighted directly from the computerised parts warehouse in Dingolfing. The huge, centralised warehouse complex at Dingolfing is the hub of BMW's world-wide parts supply system, which is divided into three levels. To handle customers' immediate needs all franchised dealers carry stocks of the most popular motor cycle parts and accessories. Major dealers or the importing company keep a total parts inventory, which includes items rarely required, and may be able to cope with models no longer in producton. This normally guarantees every BMW owner a prompt spares service wherever it is needed. To replenish stocks or to trace really obscure items the call goes out to Munich and Dingolfing. The latter is a small town on the river Isar and its history goes back over 700 years. Because of BMW it is now a leading industrial centre for Lower Bavaria. 700 people work in this ultra-modern, high-storage spares warehouse and it holds over 45,000 different items, of which about a fifth are to do with motor cycles. About 3 million spares items are handled annually using automatic selection, counting, packing and weighing machines. A remote-controlled transport system, installed in 1980, shifts parts pallets around the warehouse guided by induction cables buried in the floor. The high-storage part of the complex, where pallets are stacked over 30 m high, normally operates completely automatically. Computers with links to Munich determine all movements in the high-storage area and allocate parts to wherever storage shelves are vacant. This high degree of electronic handling and processing means that all orders are typically turned round within 24 hours. Shipment is normally by road and rail and, exceptionally, BMW will send parts by air. BMW expect to be able to provide any part for motor cycles made within the past ten years from stock and, in some cases, can meet orders for even earlier models.

BMW Motorrad relies heavily on frequent consultations with their overseas subsidiaries to make in-depth market surveys and analyses of sales trends. This information enables the Munich management to detect how different world markets vary in their sales profiles and makes it possible to set realistic sales targets and provide accurate instructions on model mix to the Berlin factory. From the same office comes the company advertising and sales literature which can be the basis for promotional activities in each of the importing countries. Analysis of warranty returns for each market helps to give early warning of component failures and prompts technical advice notes or modifications.

Although BMW does not bring forth new models with the abandon favoured by the 'big four' in Japan, by its own standards change has speeded up in recent years to keep in touch with the competition. New product development takes place in the BMW Research and Development Division, headed by Dr Karlheinz Radermacher, which is part of the parent company. Here styling exercises have been in fashion in recent years and BMW have gone outside the company to use design consultants to help with the creation of the next generation of bikes. The wind-tunnel and test track facilities at Ascheim make it possible to try out various combinations of frame geometry and engine design before proceeding to the prototype stage. Market trends have indicated the need to review its experience of turbo-charging on bikes, but the state of the art is probably still too unreliable for BMW to go ahead with road machines yet. The Barcelona Motor Show in 1981 did, however, feature a Turbo R100RS produced by Turbomecanica SA of Madrid and said to be capable of 102 bhp and 140 mph (225 km/h). More characteristic of BMW's research and development effort is the R80 G/S, which first appeared in 1980. This turned a rather hairy experimental moto-cross bike into a sophisticated vehicle for leisure sport. The best qualities from the G/S were then transformed into a full-blown road version, the R80ST.

Development work also takes place on motor cycle accessories and clothing which have considerable potential sales in a mature market. Think-tank meetings have evolved some interesting extras to tempt the discerning owner who wishes to ride dressed and equipped completely in the BMW style. One example is the BMW helmet which has a hinged chin guard which allows it to be quickly converted from an integral style to the open model favoured by off-road riders. This helmet was extensively wind-tunnel tested for streamlining and stability and it is fitted with draught-excluders and a neck-protection plate for safety and rider comfort. The fact that it is not universally available from BMW dealers serves to illustrate the problems involved in designing and manufacturing for a world market. In many instances it requires costly and time-consuming type approval tests before a product can obtain official acceptance.

The overseas shop windows for BMW bikes are the 1,800 officially recognised motor cycle dealers and their showrooms, and the various national and international exhibitions. BMW is anxious that its corporate identity stands comparison in every trade outlet and dealers are encouraged by incentive schemes to be thoroughly professional in the organisation and running of their showrooms. BMW wish to believe that their dealer network offers the owner comparable service whether it is needed in Tromso or Taranto. The fact that it is company policy to sell BMW products only through recognised dealers does make it easier to put standardised procedures into effect. Although there are still some uniquely individual dealers around, the trend is to smart and spacious showrooms with room to inspect the whole BMW range, a browsing area for genuine accessories and a boutique corner for clothing. The total effect is set off with the company colours and a BMW pylon to signpost the way to exclusivity.

The exchanges of ideas around the wider company is helped by regular meetings when staff from the importing companies are recalled to Munich for briefings and reports. Information flows from Munich in the form of company

Internal organisation of BMW Motorrad GmbH, the BMW Motor Cycle Division

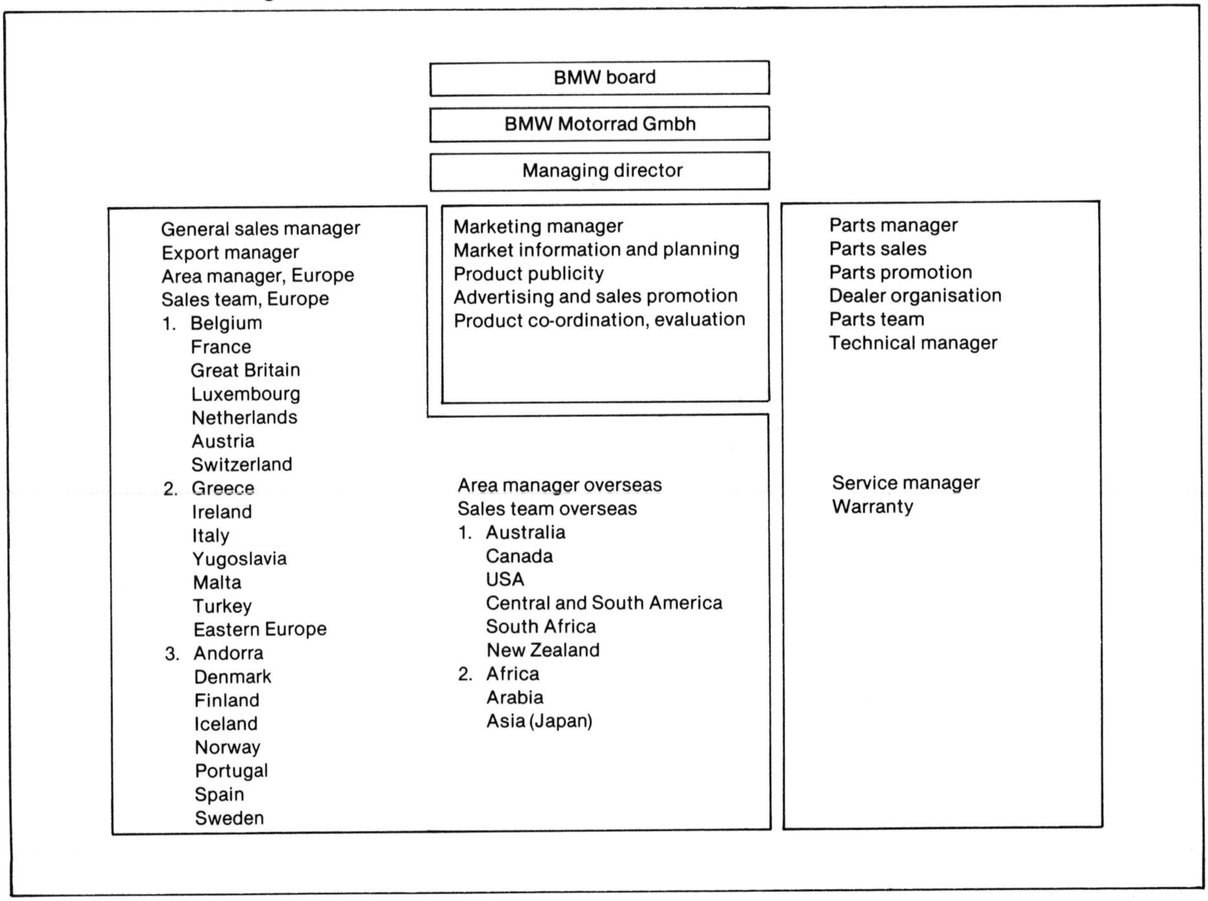

directives and visits to check out procedures or run staff development programmes. Senior staff from Germany often lend their presence to launchings and other promotional activities organised by the importing companies. BMW's international promotion team is best seen at international events such as the Isle of Man TT races where the world's motor cycle experts gather to relive past glories and to exchange views on current trade.

Viewing world motor cycle sales from Munich shows that the USA is still the No 1 overseas market, with West Germany itself the major European seller, followed by Italy, Great Britain, France and Spain. Spain is interesting in that it is the last of the big European markets which is still organised by a concession. Other significant markets are Australia, South Africa, Mexico and even Japan. In some countries, such as Brazil and Denmark, the import taxes are so prohibitive that BMW have little penetration. The continuing strength of the German mark also puts BMW at a disadvantage as it has always been company policy to manufacture only in Germany. High labour and materials costs make an overseas assembly plant in Brazil, for example, seem an attractive idea, but the Made in Germany label is seen as playing a crucial role in the marketing of BMW motor cycles.

North America presents something of a challenge because although it takes about 60 per cent of the free world's production of motor cycles it could take more BMWs. At present there are fewer than 400 BMW franchises in North America, hardly more than in France or Germany, and they are concentrated on the East and West Coasts. Major towns such as Rochester NY (population over 300,000) have no BMW dealerships and one correspondent of *BMW News*, the magazine of the BMW Motorcycle Owners of America, went as far as to describe the dealers as an endangered species! Before the Second World War the odd Beemer made it to the USA, but the domestic market was solidly devoted to the open road tourers of the Indian Company and Harley-Davidson. Just before the war Harley did produce a BMW copy for the US armed forces but the 750 cc design did not translate very efficiently into metal and the thousand odd machines which were made did not perform as expected. After the war interest in military memorabilia resulted in a number of R75 and R71 sidecar outfits being shipped back to the States where they are now proudly restored and displayed by members of the Vintage BMW Motor Cycle Owners Ltd Club. Probably the oldest BMW motor cycle still running in North America is a 1927 R42 owned by Bob Beasley.

Official importation of Beemers was started in 1949 by Victor Hardesty from Whitestone, New York. Amongst the first arrivals in May 1950 were an R24 single and two R51/2 twins which were sold by Edgewood Cycles in Maryland. Edgewood Cycles now claim in their advertising to be the oldest BMW dealers in North America. At the time of these first arrivals the most popular imported models were British BSA and Triumph. For a while the BMW importers also handled Adler two-strokes but eventually the BMW franchise passed to Alfred Bondy, a New York importer who was selling NSU motor cycles under the trading name of Butler & Smith. It was Butler & Smith who flew the flag for BMW throughout the 1960s' and 1970s' superbike revival. In the mid-'60s they gained much publicity for BMW by running a highly successful racing team and made the USA the company's best overseas market for motor cycles. During the '70s things began to get tough for the concession as aggressive Japanese marketing dominated the US bike sales and even threatened the home-grown Harley-Davidson company. By the late 1970s Munich could see that, so far as the prestigious US market was concerned, BMW was being left with a legend and the loyalty of past owners. On the sports side they could not compete with the horsepower of Kawasaki, Yamaha and Suzuki and even their famous reputation for tourers was being overtaken by Honda's Goldwing. What the Goldwing lacked in handling was more than compensated for by its price and carrying capacity. In 1975 BMW of North America Inc had been established to import and handle cars and in 1980 this wholly-owned subsidiary took over the motor cycle franchise as well.

The Butler & Smith concession then run by Dr Peter Adams did not part company from BMW with quite the same grace as accompanied the franchise takeover in Britain. The recession in motor cycle sales was already biting in the US market and BMW bike sales had dropped by 50 per cent on previous targets of up to 7,000 machines a year. Even the ailing Harley-Davidson was managing sales 15 times greater than BMW. Against a backdrop of overstocking and cut-throat discounting by the Japanese companies BMW now faced trying to re-establish the brand and bring back orderly marketing. Under the last days of the Butler & Smith franchise the dealer network had become very patchy with many small operations often offering service only. There was

The Marusho Magnum-Electra 500 (Ralph Walker).

also a problem of substantial pirating by people who were cashing in on the very high price of genuine BMW spares in North America. The first steps in this recovery programme have now been taken. Included in the first news from BMW of North America's headquarters in Montvale, NJ, have been decisions to close down almost 200 unsuitable dealerships and to reduce the prices of 500 frequently ordered motor cycle parts. The latter is clearly designed to encourage BMW owners to return to recognised BMW dealerships for their parts and service needs.

By contrast the development of a BMW subsidiary in Japan has made a flying start. In April 1981 the company took over Balcon Motors, a Panamanian-registered company that had been importing BMW cars and bikes in a small way since 1950. The idea of selling bikes to the world's greatest motor cycle makers seems, at first, somewhat perverse but the exclusivity of a BMW becomes an important selling point in such a wealthy market. For Munich there must be extra satisfaction simply from the fact of shipping genuine BMW motor cycles to Japan. After the Second World War Japan's reconstructed industry spawned over 100 small companies manufacturing motor cycles. Two of these companies, BIM and DSK, made copies of BMW's R51/3 plunger models in 250 cc and 500 cc versions with minor technical modifications to avoid infringing Munich patents. Another company, Marusha, made BMW look-alikes based on the R50/2 engine, until it folded in 1961. In 1963 it was re-organised as the Lilac Company and began producing a model called the Magnum 500. In 1966 the US Marusha Corporation was describing the Magnum ST in its advertising as the world's fastest 500 cc opposed twin. Only 860 of these bikes were made and many of them were sold in the USA where there now exists a Marusha/Lilac Owners Club. The 1967 Magnum Electra version was fitted with electric start, a cartridge type oil filter and telescopic forks which, at the time, kept it ahead of BMW in terms of technical innovation. Apparently, however, its designers forgot to include a choke control and it proved to be a difficult starter in cold weather.

The decision to go world-wide was taken by BMW at the beginning of the '70s. South Africa had the first wholly-owned subsidiary in 1972 and in ten years BMW has created 'daughter companies' in 11 important world markets: South Africa (1972), France (1972), Italy (1973), Belgium (1973), the USA (1975/1980), Switzerland (1976), Austria (1977), the Netherlands (1979), Australia (1979), Great Britain (1980) and Japan (1981). Some two-thirds of car and bike production is now exported overseas and the bulk of it is destined for the 11 major markets. Much of the huge overseas investment by BMW has been to regularise its car sales, but the motor cycle side of the business has been a willing partner because its future was seen to require the same treatment. BMW's present buoyancy as an independent and profitable concern is seen by the management as convincing justification for its expansion overseas. Independent importers could not have been a reliable means of handling the current volume of sales or that planned. Clearly, what just a few years ago was a Germany-orientated company, substantially dependent on home sales, is now one of the top international vehicle makers.

10

Concessionaires—the British experience

Until the 1970s BMW motor cycles were sold abroad through appointed concessions in each country. In turn the concession normally franchised selected dealers to stock and sell the bikes to the public. This chapter traces the evolution of the BMW concession in Britain where the Munich twins have been on sale for over half a century.

In the beginning BMW concentrated on establishing its new venture into motor cycles in the home market where competition from DKW, NSU, Victoria and Zündapp was already very strong. However, interest in this new motor cycle outside Germany was already high following its appearance at the 1923 Paris Motor Show. Subsequently, motor cycle journalists followed BMW's tentative steps on the race track, which included Schleicher's surprising gold medal win in the 1926 ISDE and the early application of supercharging. BMW exhibited at the Olympia Motor Show, London, in 1928 and it was about the same time that individual bikes were air freighted in to Heston Air Park by B.N. Aircraft Ltd. Heston was then, with Croydon, London's principal airfield and mostly handled the European air traffic. The first machines were sold through Beach Motors and Godfreys Ltd, well-known dealers in Great Portland Street, which was then the mecca of the retail motor cycle trade in London. On March 18 1931 the weekly journal, *Motor Cycling*, the famous 'green un', published a detailed road test on the R16 sports 750 which BMW had launched two years earlier. The report was extremely complimentary, describing the bike as a wonderful machine fit for the connoisseur with the means to satisfy expensive tastes. Certainly, the interest the bike seems to have aroused in passers-by while on test suggests that BMWs at this time were extremely rare on British roads.

Soon, however, British enthusiasts were able to satisfy their expensive tastes for imported German motor cycles in a more reliable fashion. In 1935 AFN Ltd, of Isleworth, began regularly importing BMW motor cycles from the factory in Munich. AFN had started in 1927 making sports cars to the design of noted early car maker Archie Frazer-Nash. Frazer-Nash, a creative designer, had started a business making GN cyclecars with Ron Godfrey before the First World War. By the 1920s the Nash works was into the limited production of chain-driven sports and touring cars. This was not a secure basis for the company and in 1927 H.J. Aldington who had once served as a GN apprentice and later a main agent for FN and GN cars in Richmond, acquired the works and the manufacturing rights. By 1930 AFN Ltd was installed in a new car works and showrooms along the London Road, Isleworth. Here, at the Falcon Works, H.J. Aldington was joined by his brothers W.H. and D.A. and they developed the TT Replica Frazer-Nash which soon gained international recognition in races and rallies abroad. The works team which included H.J. was particularly successful in the Alpine Trials and devotees of the marque talk wistfully of 'Nashing' through France and Switzerland in the '30s. In fact, it was at the 1934 Alpine Rally that AFN made its connection with BMW. It brought together a British firm famous for its chain-driven cars with a Germany company whose reputation was built on shaft-drive motor cycles!

Greatly impressed by the performance of the new type 315 BMW cars with their four-speed boxes and swinging axles, H.J. Aldington left the Rally finish at Monte Carlo and drove straight to Munich to negotiate the rights to sell these vehicles in Britain. Recognising the prestige of the Frazer-Nash name and their own rather recent reputation for four-wheelers, BMW agreed to their cars being marketed in Britain as Frazer Nash-BMWs. The combination as well-conceived and the Frazer Nash-BMW became arguably the most advanced sports car available in the '30s. At first the cars arrived in Britain with left-hand drive and required conversion at Isleworth, but later Munich sent the cars ready to be driven without modification on British roads. The success of the collaboration led BMW to ask AFN to market their other products and so the first motor cycles arrived. AFN appointed J.M. West, a well-known trialist, as motor cycle sales manager which added to the company's distinctly sporting image. The first bikes were the Star-framed R12 and R17, both equipped with very modern hydraulically-damped telescopic forks and some smaller R2 and

R4 models which did not sell so well. Early dealers to agree to sell the BMW motor cycles included Bryants of Biggleswade, Commerfords of Thames Ditton, Hull of Balham, Victor Horsman in Liverpool, King's Motors of Oxford, Laytons of Oxford and Claude Rye in Fulham. AFN kept a register of all BMW motor cycles sold and this shows some 355 sales up to the outbreak of the Second World War. Particularly popular models were the R5 in 1936 and 1937 and the R51 in 1938/39. Some bikes were shipped overseas including an R17 to L.F. Pratt who subsequently used it to win the Australian Sidecar Championships. He later went on to start the first BMW concession in Australia. It is interesting to note that the original AFN agreement with BMW was for five years, an unusually long contract, and it expressly granted the British concession a non-exclusive right to sell to the Dominions. Bikes were also sold directly from the London Road showrooms of the concessionaires where they were often fitted with Steib sidecars, a franchise AFN had taken over from Pride and Clarke of Brixton.

As befitted their sporting image, AFN took every advantage of putting their products to the test. It was an AFN belief that their cars and bikes sold on their performance and sales staff were expected and encouraged to show customers how to get the maximum output from their purchases. It took a brave customer to continue with a complaint that his car or bike was off-song or not handling properly after H.J. or Jock West had tested and approved it! H.J. raced cars at home and abroad on circuits such as Ards in Ulster and the Hamburger Park in Germany. His sales manager, Jock West, was equally busy on the motor cycle racing scene. He was a frequent entrant in the Hour High Speed Trials held at the famous Brooklands racing bowl. In 1938, on a second-hand R17, fitted with a borrowed, hand-cut front tyre, he lapped the bumpy concrete at over 100 mph (160 km/h) to win a gold medal. On another hectic occasion, in one day, he won the MCC High Speed Trial on a BMW bike and then immediately joined H.J. Aldington as his passenger for a second 100-plus mph pursuit in a Frazer Nash BMW. Jock West recalls being so tired that night, as he drove home from Weybridge, that he lost the bike and its trailer in South London without noticing they had left the back of his car. Next day the police found bike and trailer miles away in Catford where they had come unhitched and simply coasted to a halt at the side of the road!

Racing was a good way for the importer to gain publicity and from 1937 Jock West became internationally known for his exploits on the blown BMWs. His greatest coup was the double victory in the Ulster GP, but he was also a front runner on the Isle of Man and the continental circuits. The 1939 AFN advertising made full use of the Meier/West TT victories and went on to claim that BMWs were the world's fastest and finest motor cycles. H.J. Aldington himself seems to have had a very close relationship with BMW because of his racing interests and he was a frequent visitor to Munich. He was influential in bringing together the works team of Meier and West and, following Gall's tragic death in the 1939 TT, it was H.J. who finally persuaded BMW to carry on and win rather than withdraw its works team.

By 1939 AFN Ltd had created an active extension of BMW in Britain. The degree of co-operation with Munich, largely effected through Fritz Trötsch, was probably not to be equalled again until BMW created its own subsidiary company 41 years later. Sales of motor cycles had swung up dramatically in 1937 and looked like sustaining this momentum when world events suddenly brought everything to a stop. The summer 1939 advertising showed that AFN were offering the R23, R35, R51, R61, R66 and R71 models. All of them could be fitted either with the standard Steib chair or the special BMW version known as the Royal. All car and motor cycle imports from Munich ceased abruptly from August 1939. During the war years AFN's Falcon Works was commissioned as *HMS Victory V* and became a training establishment where Royal Navy mechanics worked on fast patrol boat engines. Some of AFN's experienced staff such as Nelson Ledger and Harry Olrog were switched from the draft to keep a BMW repairs and servicing agency going at Isleworth. A number of doctors and other essential personnel who had bought BMW cars before the war now required their vehicles to be kept in regular running order.

With the war over, AFN Ltd was anxious to normalise its business and re-establish its links with BMW. Germany, however, was in turmoil and in Munich the victors were gathering around the spoils. As early as November 1945 H.J. Aldington was at the war-damaged factory endorsing the petition that the BMW board made to the US military authorities against closure of the plant. While he was there he is said also to have been helpful in achieving recognition for two of BMW's pre-war superstars, Georg Meier and Ernst Henne. Henne was working as a nightwatchman on an American airbase and Meier was facing difficulties with the military authorities over his honorary Army ranks acquired through his pre-war racing successes.

For two years the Aldington brothers battled with bureaucracy and the chaos in Germany to salvage something from the wreck. There was the matter of orders and invoices not cleared by BMW before the war interrupted things. A special interest of H.J. was the safe return of his 'White Racer', GMV 618, a competition type 328 model which had been in the Munich factory on the outbreak of hostilities for crash repairs following a shunt at the Hamburg Park race track. There was also a major interest in trying to acquire commercially useful plans, machine tools, parts and engines, which it was proposed to share with the Bristol Aeroplane Company in a peacetime scheme to produce BMW type sports cars. In this respect, AFN was pursuing the sort of entrepreneurial initiative that the Allied command were encouraging in order to take commercial advantage of Germany's defeat. The BMW factory had quickly lost its development rig for testing high-altitude aero engines and Munich airfield was busy at this time with the air freighting of crates to the USA and England. The Aldington brothers were certainly part of an 'official' investigation team authorised by the British Ministry of Supply, and a cloak and dagger story certainly exists of a Stirling bomber making a secret flight between the curfewed city of Munich and Filton, Bristol.

The outcome of this messy period is more precisely known and recognised. Eugene Keller Jr's order to dismantle the BMW factory was not implemented. Instead permission was granted to restart limited peacetime work although, fortunately, not under the proposed new company name of the Bayerische Erzeugnungswerke—it would have hardly fitted the princess BMW was to become! BMW 328 engines, parts and designs did find their way to Bristol and AFN Ltd, along with company designer Dr Fiedler. Car enthusiasts will recognise the outcome of this Anglo-German alliance in the Bristol 400 and the very successful Frazer-Nash racers of the '50s which used a development of the type 328 engine. H.J. Aldington eventually got back his car, GMV 618, although mysteriously, during its absence abroad, it had adopted a Mille Miglia type body shell and switched from right to left-hand drive! Georg Meier was soon back in the saddle winning races on the supercharged BMW bikes.

AFN's immediate efforts after the war were

The BMW/AFN stand at Olympia in 1936. W.H. Aldington, Director of AFN Ltd on the left admires Henne's 1935 record-breaking 750 and BMW Export Manager, Fritz Trotsch, admires the camera work (AFN Ltd—W.H. Aldington collection).

devoted mainly to developing the 328 engine. Jock West did not return to AFN, moving instead to AMC at Plumstead, but he did race again in the 1947 and 1948 TT and in Ulster. For a while the BMW-engined Frazer-Nash cars were a considerable force on the race tracks. In 1948 a High Speed model driven by H.J. Aldington and Norman Culpan came third at Le Mans. In 1951 Franco Cortese drove a Nash to the first British victory ever in the tough Targa Florio in Sicily. Famous drivers such as Stirling Moss, Mike Hawthorn, Ken Wharton and Dick Seaman were consistently successful in these hand-built sports cars before they faded from the spotlight at the close of the '50s. Back at the Falcon Works *HMS Victory V* had been paid off and BMW servicing and repairs expanded. Motor cycle imports from Germany did not officially restart until 1951 and with the British market flooded with war-surplus machines of every sort there was little incentive to push the two-wheel side of the business.

Slowly new BMW motor cycles became available in Britain once Munich re-started making twins in 1950. The first arrivals were the 500 cc R51/2/3 and the R67 which was often fitted with a Steib sidecar. The special relationship between AFN Ltd and BMW of pre-war days was no longer in evidence and this encouraged Charles Lock, an ex-AFN apprentice and freshly

The 1955 R67 with heavy-duty TR 500 sidecar (BMW).

demobbed, to start his own BMW motor cycle repair workshop. Joining forces with two friends, Vincent Motler and James Gregory, Charlie Lock created MLG in 1949 and became AFN's first post-war BMW agency. There were so few BMWs in those days in Britain that MLG quickly became almost a BMW owners club. Virtually every owner and BMW motor cycle in the country were known to the MLG staff and, at some stage, passed through their workshop. At first this was in a disused air raid shelter, but later spread along Goldhawk Mews in West London to become a mecca for BMW enthusiasts from all over the country. Genuine parts were still acutely short and Vin Motler's skill as a machine tool setter was useful for making up hard-to-find bushes and valve guides. Alf Cook, still working for MLG, recalls the workshop remaining open late at night to get stranded BMW owners back on the road. Once he even made a correct diagnosis of a sticking exhaust valve on a BMW for an owner, a long distance away and unable to get to the workshop, by listening to the bike over the telephone!

A friendship with Georg Meier, who had himself set up a large BMW agency in Munich, helped Charles Lock get on a factory course for the R51/2. In 1951 MLG became AFN's official service agency specialising in frame and crankshaft repairs. The high price of BMW bikes deterred most dealers from stocking them but new names, such as Coombes of Slough and Slocombes at Neasden, did handle some sales and servicing. For a while MLG acted, in effect, as an extension to the importers, AFN, so far as bikes were concerned. They carried out most of the warranty work on new bikes and their racing team created a good deal of publicity for BMW. It was also MLG which obtained authentic-looking Wehrmacht machines for British-made films about the Second World War. An R51/3 (1951) starred in *Carve Her Name with Pride* and the television series *Moonstrike* featured a 1955 R26! MLG was eventually forced to give up racing and later still, in 1970, concentrated entirely on car sales at their Chiswick High Road showrooms. Their enthusiasm for BMW motor cycles did set a high standard of service which was later to be followed by dealerships such as Gus Kuhn in South London and Hughenden M40 near Oxford.

BMW showed motor cycles again at Olympia in 1951. AFN Ltd found its BMW connections much harder going with an aging range of bikes which were not competitively priced and an odd selection of car models. The ultra-exclusive eight-cylinder models (types 502/3) offered limited sales potential at a time when living standards generally were only slowly recovering from the disruptions of wartime. One of their best sellers was the Steib sidecar and as many as 350 chairs a year were leaving their workshops as often fitted to British bikes as to BMWs. The fashion for three-wheelers was, however, about to change and, when Steib gave up sidecar manufacture in 1957, AFN found itself diversifying into the sale of agricultural muck spreaders. In 1953 AFN took on the Porsche concession which began the long and successful association which continues to the present. In 1954 it added the DKW concession and began importing the Hobby scooter. Later, during the Suez Crisis and petrol rationing in Britain, these scooters were being imported from the French licence holders, Manurhin of Paris.

BMW itself was going through its difficult patch at this time and all it could offer AFN was the Isetta bubble car. AFN reluctantly handled this odd three-wheeler but the fall from grace was substantial and, when BMW decided to seek a manufacturer in Britain for the stretched 600 version, H.J. Aldington was not unhappy about offering the chance to the rest of the trade. Whereas the original BMW 500 was a true three-wheeler which could be driven in Britain on a motor cycle licence, the 600 model had a duplex rear wheel drive and was taxed as a car. The contract was first offered to Standard Cars, which had links with AFN, but it was the ailing Armstrong Siddeley Company which showed greater interest. Armstrong became insolvent and it was one of its directors, an ex-airline pilot, Captain Ron Ashley, who stepped into the vacuum and established an assembly line in the old railway works at Brighton. Despite BMW support, Isetta (GB) Ltd was not to succeed. The BMW 600 was a short-lived phenomenon in Britain. It was not as cute as the true bubble cars, it handled badly on its close-together rear wheels and the strange, off-side lateral passenger door certainly did not find favour with the British public. For AFN the concession finally ended in 1962 when BMW declined to guarantee it the right to handle the new 700 series car. The BMW concession in Great Britain was about to start a period of rapid and unsettling change and mobility.

In September 1962 Isetta (GB) Ltd was put into the hands of the official receiver and the remains were bought up by Glanfield Lawrence, a long-established trading group with car and motor cycle outlets retailing in Southern England. It had already been handling BMW motor cycles and the Isetta bubble cars at its Highbury, London depot and the purchase of Isetta (GB) secured its spares supply. The BMW concession brought with it the new 700 series cars and these were prepared for sale at the Brighton works. Back into the picture came Jock West as director and general manager and he quickly devoted himself to re-building the motor cycle imports. The bike side of the business was handled from new premises at Portslade in Hove and sales gradually picked up to about 200. In 1964 the 1800 series cars began to arrive and BMW was looking to the concession to invest in expansion. As a public company, Glanfield Lawrence felt unable to take orders from BMW and, in August 1965, the concession was passed over to the Chipstead Motor Group. Glanfield Lawrence remained a source of Isetta spares until 1978 and now its Brighton depot handles imports of Italian light diesel engines and chain saws.

The Chipstead Motor Group was owned by ex-racing driver Jonathan Sieff, one of the Marks & Spencer family, and the capital for the new concession was provided by Vistby Finance. Chipstead also held the concession for Maserati and Moskvitch cars and was the London distributor for Alfa Romeo. The Chipstead showrooms now added the distinctively styled BMW four-cylinder saloons and coupes, which were to set Munich once more on the path of expansion and profitability. Primarily car

The BMW 600. Even converted to right-hand drive there remained the problem of the off-side door! (AFN Ltd—the W.H. Aldington collection).

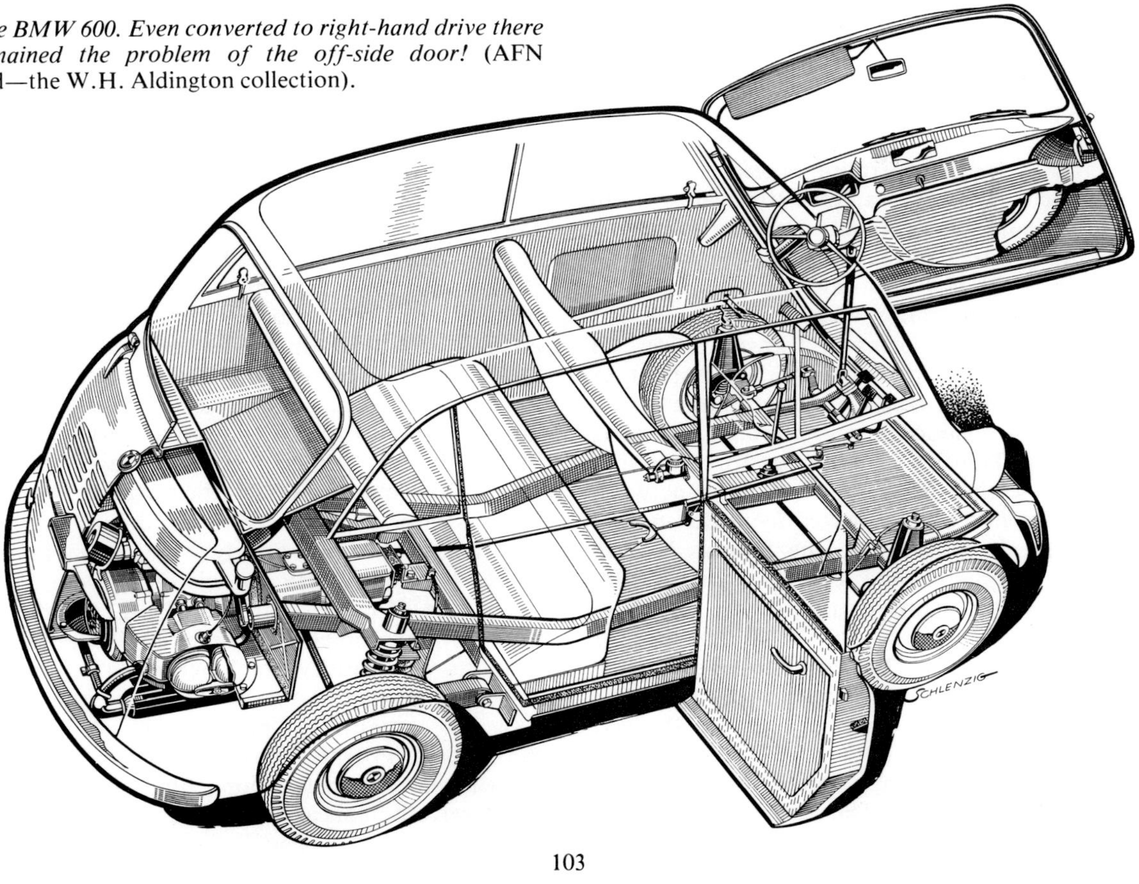

retailers, Chipstead had little interest in the motor cycles and Glanfield Lawrence was asked to keep that side of the concession ticking over. This was not easy, however, as high prices made worse by steep import surcharges made the BMWs uncompetitive against the surging waves of the Japanese sales. Eventually, the motley collection of franchises was rationalised and the responsibility for BMW cars shifted to Cooper Cars which had showrooms in Bournemouth, Leicester and London. Cooper Cars still operates the best known BMW dealerships in Britain, including the prestigiously-sited Park Lane showroom, often thought by many to be BMW's British headquarters. The motor cycles remained a minor side of the business with sales to special order sometimes through the car showrooms. As the '60s came to a close, wartime apart, sales of BMW motor cycles in Britain were probably at their lowest ebb since imports had begun. The waiting time for a new bike was anything up to six months and supplies were drying up with the company switching production to Berlin. At a time when a Triumph Bonneville could be purchased for £350, an R60 retailed at £750. The small band of British BMW owners found the concession increasingly hard-pressed to satisfy their needs for spare parts and service.

Change was coming and the '70s heralded a new deal for BMW motor cycles in Great Britain. As car sales were doing so well, BMW decided that its other products needed the same vigorous marketing. The new generation bikes were now on stream and BMW was in a much stronger position to join the superbike revival which was gathering momentum. The chance arose from the arrival on the scene of Tozer, Kemsley and Millbourn, a large finance corporation with extensive interests in shipping and all forms of transportation. In their first year of the concession TKM spent £5 million establishing BMW Concessionaires (UK) Ltd, and this included a new imports and parts warehouse in Dover. A small sales force scoured the country setting up a revitalised dealer network to handle the new bikes expected from Berlin. The first recruit was Gus Kuhn, the famous Norton dealer in Clapham, and the 18-strong dealer network included many of the dealers who had been carrying the torch for BMW during the darker post-war days. The new concession created a separate motor cycle division and moved bike operations from the South Coast to Byfleet, Surrey. The message about BMW motor cycles was shortly to be put across, loudly and clearly, to the British biking public. The old hands with their classic BMW models were about to be joined by a whole new generation of bikers riding the new-style Bavarian twins.

The motor cycle division of the new concession was run by a small force of dedicated and talented sales people. What they lacked in product experience they overcame by their sheer determination to sell. Their style included all the razzmatazz of modern marketing techniques and began with, as is now standard practice, a presentation and launch. This took place at the Tower Hotel in London in January 1971 with the dealers and the motor cycle Press being introduced to the Stroke 5 range. Variety star Danny La Rue, one of a number of famous personalities to have owned and ridden BMW motor cycles, added colour to the proceedings although behind the scenes the event had nearly become a farce. As few of the TKM staff had motor cycle riding experience, the bikes were brought to the presentation in a furniture lorry. The lorry had got lost in London's traffic and the driver's difficulties were made worse by the fact that the hotel had only just recently changed its name. When the bikes finally arrived, cleverly arranged on display trailers, it was discovered that the hotel lifts were too small to take them to the top floor suite where the Press and the dealers were starting anxiously to look for them. Superhuman strength, borne of desperation and panic, manhandled the bikes, standing vertically on their rear wheels, into the lifts and eventually to an enthusiastically-attended reception.

By 1972 this inspired team work had pushed sales of bikes to over 200 units a year and the dealer network stretched from Ayrshire to Bridgend to Ipswich. Smees Advertising had been brought in to put a professional emphasis to the image re-building which was designed to support local dealers' efforts. Top society photographer, Patrick Lichfield, was used to provide glossy images of power to put across the spirit of biking the BMW way. Dealers were encouraged to stock at least four machines from the range and to run a demonstrator so that buyers could get first-hand experience of how utterly safe, reliable and comfortable the BMW models really were. For a generation of bikers reared on BSA, Honda and Triumph superbikes these new BMWs presented an unknown quantity which needed to be sampled to be appreciated. Another marketing innovation was to organise Open Days at dealers' showrooms. Potential buyers would be wooed by extra local advertising, opportunities to ride test bikes, refreshments and a chance to talk shop.

Typical advertising by the British concession in the 1970s firmly linking BMW ownership with the corridors of power (Patrick Lichfield).

Sales doubled again in 1973, although the fuel crisis of that year was a set-back for the car side of the business. The BMW motor cycle dealer network had grown to nearly 40 and it was projected as reaching 100. The motor cycle division team had grown from three to seven by 1974 when the headquarters was switched to Chiswick in West London. A considerable boost to business resulted about this time from the large sales of motor cycles to British police forces. By 1976 the volume sales to the Metropolitan Police were being delivered and the public was getting used to seeing the smart new bikes on road patrol duties. These sales were good for business but the decision to handle public authority business directly from the concession did not please dealers who saw a lucrative local trade arrangement denied to them.

Another group not particularly pleased by the new concession's style were the old guard members of the owners club. High-pressure marketing was making ownership of BMW motor cycles less exclusive and the frequent arrival of fresh models meant that the importers seemed less concerned for the sales already made than the sales which were expected to come. Nor did the concession seem favourably disposed towards the club's requests for special discounts and its practice of advertising sources of cheap spares from the continent. It was in everyone's interests to maintain good relationships but some mutual suspicions lingered on. The enthusiasts who had seen the difficult times saw the concession as a lot of brash whizz-kids who were unsympathetic to the real values of biking, while club members were sometimes dismissed by Chiswick as a bunch of fanatics dedicated to past glories. It is clearer now that biking at that time was facing a revolution in the way in which it was being marketed. The trend was already away from the friendly corner shop operation, run by enthusiasts for enthusiasts, to a professional form of selling where sales graphs and targets were all-important. Inevitably as the concession grew in size it became more difficult to deal in personalities.

Meantime BMW Concessionaires (GB) continued with its lively methods of shifting metal. The 1976 Road Show was a classic of its time, touring Britain with coloured lights, misty smoke, music and exotically-clad girls to launch the new RS model. It was, in the jargon of those times, a mind-blowing experience for dealers and visitors, and in total contrast to the somewhat staid official launch by the company at the Frankfurt Motor Show. The concession encouraged publicity-creating events such as the Maudes Trophy attempt in 1973 and encouraged dealer sponsorship such as the Gus Kuhn Racing Team and Penthouse racers. In 1977 a major event for dealers and the media was the first BMW Rideaway. Forty dealers were taken to Munich to pick up new red R100RS machines which were then ridden back to England in convoy. Such events and lavish Press launchings in far-off places such as Monte Carlo and Spain gave the concession something of a reputation for style and flair. It might have raised a few eyebrows in Munich but BMW must have been delighted by the continued rise in sales. By 1977 sales were over 1,700 machines a year and in 1979, the last year of the TKM concession, the sales graph nudged over 2,800 units.

The concession was clearly very healthy both on the car side and with the motor cycles. TKM had seen a profit and they had used the right people fully to exploit it. Its contract to handle BMW products was fixed and it was clearly company policy that it would eventually convert the operation to a wholly-owned subsidiary. Only a few of the TKM staff switched to BMW (GB) Ltd and a number took their experience to the Japanese Colt Car Company which was getting itself established in Britain. It had been a lively period in the history of the BMW concession in

Britain and, in the words of Richard Styer, once BMW Motor Cycle Division General Manager and now MD of Colt Cars, 'It was a pleasure to work with such a team'. For a short period TKM kept an interest in motor cycles by taking over, as a replacement for BMW, the Benelli franchise.

Thus it was in January 1980 that Germany established BMW (GB) Ltd at Bracknell in Berkshire. The staff were settled into a smart and distinguished new office and warehouse complex some 30 miles west of London which had cost £7½ million to build. Bracknell had been chosen because it was a green-field site with New Town facilities and excellent motorway connections. It had also already attracted other up-market manufacturers, particularly in the computer business, such as Sperry and ICL. For BMW it enabled them to put the whole British operation, which previously had been split between Brentford and Chiswick, under one roof. The new building presented a shining example of BMW's recently born corporate identity. The new Motor Cycle Division was headed by Pat Myers who had come from Volkswagen Cars and technical continuity was provided by Alberto Criscuolo whose experience goes back to the days of the Chipstead Motor Group.

Being a wholly-owned subsidiary BMW (GB) Ltd is now more clearly controlled from Munich but, in several ways, it can operate as an independent agent. Its chief responsibility is to be profitable and Munich has delegated considerable freedom of action in the best way to run the business. It is very much a car marketing organisation with motor cycles and marine engines providing a significant but minor contribution to overall profits. The present Managing Director is Dr Walter Hasselkus who was running BMW's Berlin operations and replaced Herr Wagner who supervised the initial creation of the company's eighth subsidiary at Bracknell. BMW sales targets for the start of the '80s are expected to reach 20,000 cars and 3,000 motor cycles which will see an increase of about a third on the figures reached by the concession. Certainly, the first signs are that the parent company in Munich must be satisfied by the smooth takeover in what has become one of their top export markets.

The motor cycle dealer network has now reached 85 and this may slowly climb towards 100. Eastern England remains an area where more dealers might be found. The country is divided into five sales territories to service and supervise dealers' requirements. Each dealer is granted an exclusive area of sales responsibility in return for meeting specified stocking levels and equipment standards. Compared with the trade generally, the BMW dealer contract yields higher than average profit margins and is very positive about forbidding discount selling. It guarantees dealers a high level of sales and technical back-up in recognition of the substantial financial commitment which running a BMW dealership entails. It is estimated that to set up an 'A' type dealership with exclusive area sales of BMW motor cycles would cost, in 1981, approaching £25,000. Unlike in Germany, BMW dealers in Britain tend to handle either cars or bikes. Only 11 joint dealerships operate in this country, although in Germany at least half are combined. In Germany the events of history meant that it was the early bike dealers, such as Theo Schoth in Berlin and Otto Artmaier in Salzburg, who were asked to add cars to their showrooms when BMW first started manufacture of four-wheelers. In Britain it has usually been found that car and motor cycle customers do not happily mix and the sales organisations have been kept quite separate. Exclusive franchises are even rarer and Britain is typical of all the major importing countries in selling mostly through multi-franchise dealers. The best known solus BMW dealership in Britain is Hughenden M40, although in 1972 Gus Kuhn opened their BMW Centre and claimed it was the only solus franchise for motor cycles in the whole of Europe.

The Motor Cycle Division at Bracknell is a typically small working team. An important function is the organisation of the sales and service field force which co-ordinates the dealers' needs and ensures that showrooms are always appropriately stocked with BMW products. Much of the day at Bracknell is spent in hectic dealings with everyday enquiries about BMW motor cycles. From the dealers came requests for technical information, orders for spares and new machines, warranty issues and suggestions for supporting local promotional activities. The public may phone in with queries about the model range, its price and its capabilities. The motor cycle Press are always keen to be kept up to date with developments and they may be seeking clarification over technical matters. At the same time there are important matters of policy and planning to be settled. The constant challenge for the importing company is to achieve a workable balance between the needs of the company to produce motor cycles and the abilities of the dealer network to sell them. This places the Bracknell team in a vital information gathering and processing position. From one

The Gus Kuhn BMW Centre on its official opening in December 1971. The J-registered Stroke 5 machine is fitted with one of the typical heavy fairings of those times (Vincent Davey).

viewpoint this involves persuading dealers to do their best with what the company is currently producing and this requires not only marketing and promotion, but dealer education and training. In the other direction they must be able to supply the company with an accurate picture of what the national market needs and what it might be able to stand.

Many of the services provided at Bracknell are used jointly by both the car and the motor cycle sides of the business. Because BMWs are sold to a demanding public, sales people from the dealers are trained to know their bikes and understand how to make a sale. They also have ways to keep customers loyal and happy. The training facilities include an elaborately laid out workshop for product knowledge training and developing technical skills. Mechanics who successfully complete these courses are awarded certificates of competence to service BMW motor cycles. A recent introduction at Bracknell has been the Motor Cycle Parts Guild whose fellowship may be awarded to parts managers able to complete a written examination and an interview designed to test their understanding of the BMW parts business. The Guild certificate already has standing in the car world and it is a further sign of the increasing professionalism in the bike side of the business.

The warehouse at Bracknell stores about £11 million worth of car and motor cycle spares, enough for four months' normal demand. Some £2 million worth of this is made up of motor cycle parts. The 100,000 sq ft (9,300 sq m) of warehouse space has 33,000 pallet locations which can take 1.8 million different parts. Over 250,000 items a month enter and leave this treasure chest of genuine BMW parts. Dealers raise orders for parts through a telephone sales system which has computer linkage to give immediate notification of stock availability. Visual display units can indicate whether a part is in stock at Bracknell, in transit through Harwich from Dingolfing or needs to be ordered from Germany. From Bracknell parts are distributed to dealers by a fleet of five National Carriers vehicles in BMW livery. BMW (GB) take pride in the speed with which parts orders are processed and even an order raised through Germany would normally only take three weeks from the time of the initial request to fitting by the dealer. BMW have standardised on IBM computers and improvements in the flow of world-wide data make it possible to forecast what levels of stocks need to be kept and whether failure rates are becoming unacceptably high and

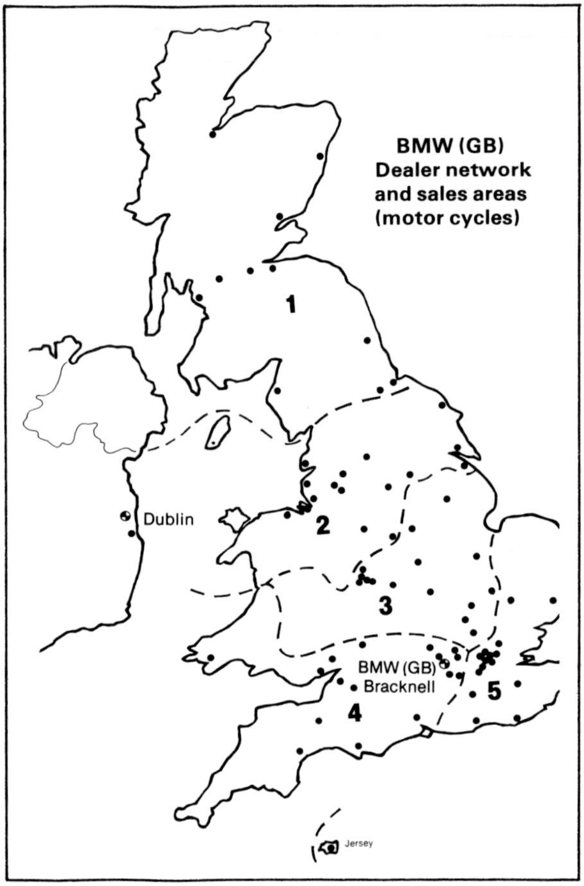

require investigation. The seasonal demand for parts usually shows a peak in the month of June which is roughly double the levels experienced during the slack month of January. The demand for panniers recently showed the following pattern over a 12 month period:

May	*Jun*	*Jul*	*Aug*	*Sep*	*Oct*	*Nov*	*Dec*	*Jan*	*Feb*	*Mar*	*Apr*
192	186	237	156	165	87	35	50	75	72	146	232

Apart from providing a flow of specialist advice and information between the factory and the dealers, the technical section is also concerned to keep track of any manufacturing defects in BMW products. This involves liaison with the warranty claims department, known in the business as the 'dustbin'. BMW motor cycles are guaranteed unconditionally for 12 months and unlimited mileage and the trade generally recognises the BMW warranty as amongst the best. Computer records now make it possible to create an international warranty system which validates claims by comparison with typical failure rates around the world.

Getting the marketing strategy right plays a key part in keeping the importing company in profit. Orderly marketing requires accurate forward planning and this makes it important for dealers to achieve set targets for new machine sales, parts and accessories. The factory needs accurate estimates of the likely model mix demand so that

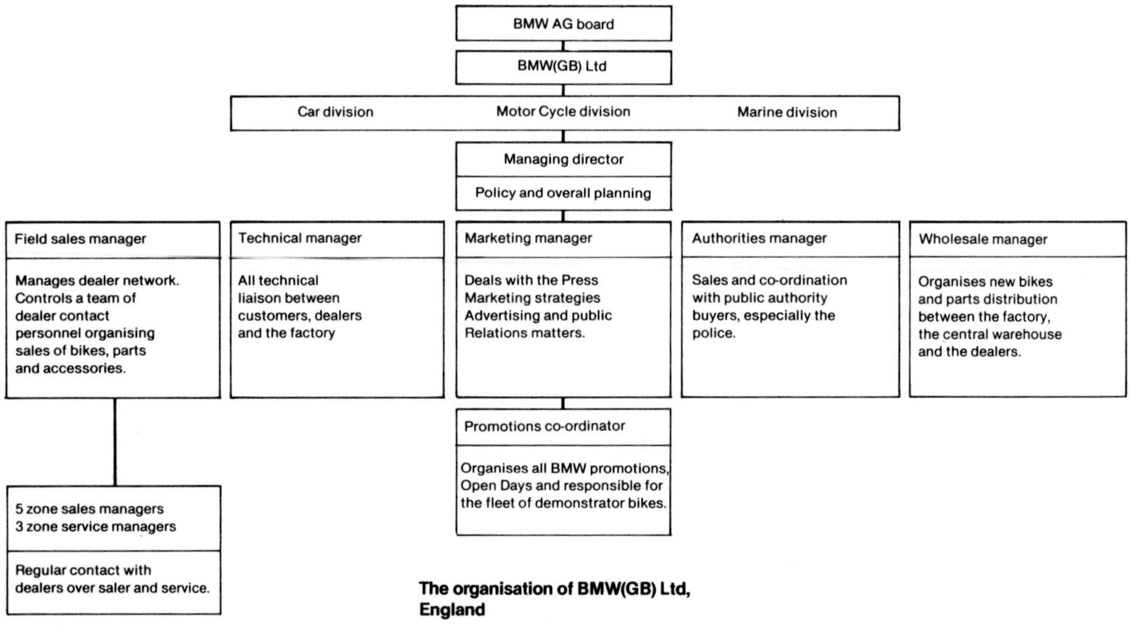

The organisation of BMW(GB) Ltd, England

production can be planned properly, although some flexibility is now possible because BMW controls so many of its own importing companies. An important marketing decision for the importing company is to fix the level of prices for BMW motor cycles which are not standardised in Europe let alone the rest of the world. Pricing policy, along with advertising and special inducements such as subsidised finance schemes, can be used to move backlogs where a particular model is not selling as expected. BMW (GB) use the London public relations agency, White, Rutherford and Scott to advise generally on the best way to spend the advertising budget to achieve maximum exposure for motor cycles. The 1982 advertising proposals include not only orthodox exposure in the motor cycle journals but a plan to use giant roadside posters which will display to passing motorists something of the excitement of biking the BMW way. The marketing section at Bracknell also runs a fleet of demonstrators which are loaned out for road tests by the major motor cycle magazines and used for promotional activities at open days, exhibitions and national rallies.

Twenty years ago the BMW story seemed to be in its final chapter. The extent of its presence overseas was more of a legend than a reality. Astonishingly the company picked itself up from the floor unaided and drove itself back into profits. The keys to this comeback were hard work and the technical flair of products such as the 1500 saloon and the motor cycles such as the R100RS. The success of BMW's marketing policies since then has turned the company into a high volume exporter and continuing high profits depend on appropriate management of its overseas markets. The British experience has shown that an overseas concession is capable of matching BMW's growth rate and the fact that the company moved rather slowly in taking over the British operation is presumably a tribute to its success. In the present tough trading times the advantages of going wholly independent in the major markets seem overwhelming. BMW (GB) has already shown in its brief running-in period so far that this pattern of sales organisation is flexible and dependable. When the upturn comes, apart from needing further expansion at Bracknell, which is already under some pressure, the parent/daughter connection will be close and caring enough to keep BMW at the top.

11

The dealer network

The BMW story starts for most bikers when they linger too long at their local dealers. In most of their showrooms the display stands alone by reason of its exclusive reputation, the attraction of its fine engineering and finish or the sheer audacity of its price. Whenever a biker enters a dealer's showrooms, whatever the prior intentions, some time will be spent on inspecting the BMW line up. The dealer, of course, is in the front line as an extension of the company and it is essential that the right kind of impression is made on all potential customers. It is here where the sales and service really have to happen.

Somewhere towards the 21st floor of the BMW *Vierzylinder* in Munich there is undoubtedly a thick file containing the blueprint for the perfect motor cycle dealership. It would be a logical conclusion to the total research effort which is directed not only at getting the product right but improving all aspects of sales organisation from the factory to the importing companies, to the after-sales, to the customer. This perfect dealer will probably be a biking enthusiast for, unlike many BMW car buyers, motor cyclists tend to be knowledgeable about what they want and expect facts rather than gloss from a salesperson. It is entirely in keeping that many of the dealerships are run by names which have become famous in racing competition or on the record tracks. Riders such as Schorsch Meier and Sebastian Nachtmann in Munich, Reg Pridmore in Ventura, California, or Freddie Frith, Tony Jefferies and George White in Britain. Flair on two wheels must also be accompanied by shrewd business sense which can organise a dealership in the professional style that has come to be the hallmark of BMW. BMW owners are not unique in expecting professional service from dealers, but they will be amongst the first to be impressed by it when it is there and certainly amongst the quickest to criticise, when it is not.

The ideal showrooms will be well-placed to act as a magnet for customers and large enough to display the entire BMW range of bikes and accessories, provide a well-equipped service area and cater for off-road parking. The building will be instantly recognisable in the house colours of white and blue with the famous BMW logo prominently positioned on an eye-catching pylon. Inside BMW bikes will occupy the best point-of-sale position and there will be an attractive display of genuine accessories and a clothing boutique. Behind the scenes a well-stocked parts section will have instant computerised links with the importers to ensure a first-class level of spares availability. The reception area will be clean and interesting and furnished with chairs, somewhere to store riding gear and perhaps refreshment facilities. Rolls of honour on the walls will display the qualifications of the staff to reassure customers that their machines are going to be in skilled hands. A spare courtesy bike will be available to loan or rent to customers when servicing leaves them temporarily without transport. Service records will be maintained as a matter of course on all customers' bikes and a full report of what has been done to the machine will be available after a service or repair job. All customers will be known by name and kept regularly informed by newsletter of promotions, special offers and service reminders. Sales will always involve extended test rides, technical and riders' reports and a detailed break-down of the services which the dealer can offer and the accessories which are provided for the model being purchased. Sales paperwork would be completed in a proper office suite furnished to the standard which matches such a high-value purchase. Here finance, warranty protection and insurance matters, all designed to benefit the BMW customer, would be swiftly settled in a business-like fashion. The total effect would be aimed at making a 'good deal', satisfying dealer and customer.

This idealistic view emphasises the key marketing function of the dealer. It makes it clear that the 'sheer riding pleasure' afforded by BMW ownership stands or falls with the dealer. Dealers should try to understand the customers' needs and attempt to establish a relationship of mutual respect and trust. A poor dealer who gives inferior service is soon known around a tightly-knit group such as bikers because of their frequent practice of making comparisons and swopping experiences. For BMW any hint of criticism is made worse by the pretentious price of purchase and the long tradition of claiming to be safe, reliable and simply the best there is. BMW more than most motor cycle manufacturers has further to fall and more face to lose. The correspondence pages of motor cycle magazines or the journals of the BMW clubs show that the owners are proud to acknowledge top class service from dealers and importers, but they can be devastating when problems occur. The enthusiast will get anxious whenever a dealer's incompetence presents any sort of threat to his dream machine, and the executive owner, unable to suffer fools lightly, will be intolerant of inefficiency or mistakes. A bike which is not ready when it should be, not serviced properly according to instructions, requires further rectification after service or is returned with chipped or greasy paintwork, immediately suggests negligence and harms a dealer's standing.

The difficulty for BMW and its importing companies lies in getting the aim of the perfect dealer accepted in all showrooms. Because most dealers are multi-franchise operations, BMW must compete with the popular makes for limited showroom space. Some of the older 'Ma and Pa' type dealerships are very small and can only offer a restricted range of models and a fraction of the total service possible. Typically with such dealers the showroom is a confusion of bikes, the new with the trade-ins, and often spilling out on to the pavement in front of the cramped little shop. Viewing a bike is not easy and may involve climbing across a muddle of machines or paint-crunching manoeuvres to get the object of one's desire out in the open. Each night the bikes are herded together completely filling the shop floor bumper to bumper. Every morning an intricate moving ritual is necessary to make space for the customers or to let the staff get into the shop! Buying can mean a longish wait at the high, coffee-stained counter with its battered and oily parts catalogues while staff get on with their work.

The 'Schorsch' Meier showrooms in Munich (BMW).

This will involve long 'phone calls, deep plunges into the nuts and bolts containers, helping the mechanic out road-testing or assembling a Japanese lightweight from a heap of parts spread across the only free space on the showroom floor. The talk, when it comes, is all rather technical and new customers might be deterred by the rather exclusive social club atmosphere of first names, favours and special arrangements. At the back, mechanics perform wonders of engineering in an astonishingly cramped workshop where they must spend much of their time in machine manhandling. Once the customer has become a regular the service from such dealerships can be wonderfully friendly and expert, but it can quickly become casual and unreliable because of its extreme informality.

Some dealers forego some of the profit opportunity available from a professional approach to marketing because they see it as cold and impersonal. They see running a showroom as little more than an extension of their hobby and they prefer swapping reminiscences with their customers rather than pushing sales and maximising the profit plan. This approach to business is clearly unattractive to both manufacturer and importer for whom the name of the game now is 'moving metal' and reaching unit targets.

By comparison with the major world manufacturers of motor cycles BMW's dealer networks are small, exclusive and hence rather deliberately selected. In Britain, for example, there are over 3,000 motor cycle dealerships of which only 85 handle BMW machines. Japan has 5,000 agencies of which a half carry Honda and a mere 26 stock the BMW range. Experience with car sales has established a sales organisation pattern which the motor cycle side of the business is expected to match and this policy has forced BMW to adopt a more extended role in the distribution and orderly marketing of bikes. Since taking over the USA concession from Butler & Smith, for example, BMW has trimmed its dealer network in the States by approaching 200. This has involved withdrawing the franchise from dealers unable or unwilling to provide the full range of services which has been established as a minimum standard of acceptability. Dealer education is seen as an important function of the importing companies and is achieved through conventions, short courses and by regular contact between dealers and field representatives. BMW are unusual in the motor cycling world in operating car-style agreements with their dealers.

Left *George White's BMW showrooms in Swindon during a BMW Open Day* (Author).

Below left *Slocombe's of Neasden handing over an R100RS for Bodie of the TV series, 'The Professionals'. Slocombe's experience goes back to the days when British bikes filled the showrooms* (BMW GB).

These agreements guarantee a clearly-defined sales territory, stable discount structures and valuable security of tenure. The responsibilities of the arrangement give dealer and importer a mutual stake in achieving target sales and provide BMW with a firmer control over the marketing of their bikes.

This type of contract enables dealers to build up their sales area with confidence and yields higher than average profit margins, but it does also involve a high level of investment and require a strong commitment to an exclusive rather than mass market. The days are gone when a dealer could set up quite independently with a crate of bikes, an enthusiasm for two wheels, an old shop and a bank overdraft. Yet, for many of today's successful dealers, their start in life began in such a precarious and unplanned fashion. Typical, perhaps was Slocombes of Neasden, London, and now one of BMW (GB)'s most experienced and respected dealerships. Bill Slocombe recalls getting into the trade in 1937 by selling a neighbour's Scott machine for £18 through an advertisement in the *Motor Cycle* magazine. The buyer lived in Banbury and demanded delivery to his doorstep! Gus Kuhn Motors started in 1932 from a small cycle repair shop near Clapham Common and Gus Kuhn built up the business while still captain of the Stamford Bridge Speedway Team and carrying out a successful international racing calendar.

A British dealership which closely parallels the BMW ideal is Hughenden M40 at Milton Common, Buckinghamshire. This began life as a satellite of Hughenden Motors in neighbouring High Wycombe which held a franchise for BMW cars, but had, in 1973, started selling Stroke 5 bikes. Unless the tradition is well-established as in Germany, it is difficult to sell bikes and cars together. Bikes do not compete very well with cars for floor space, the selling techniques are not the same and, particularly in Britain, the characteristic appearance of some bikers looks out

Above left *Hughenden M40 just off the M40 motorway at Milton Common* (Author).

Left *Unloading a delivery of BMW motor cycles at Hughenden M40* (Two Wheeler Dealer).

of place with the glossy and polished image of the high performance car market. Accordingly, the bike sales were soon transferred to a car garage which had become empty at the Oxford end of the new M40 motorway. The early days were a struggle as the sales figures show: 1974, 9; 1975, 15; 1976, 31; 1977, 40; 1978, 47; 1979, 53; 1980, 103.

In 1976 Ron Slater, who runs the motor cycle side of the Hughenden operation with a great flair for publicity and image-building, launched into grass track sponsorship with the R90S sidecar outfit. In 1977 planning permission was received to extend the workshop area and a Yamaha agency was started. It was, however, the workshop operation which proved to be the most profitable development and it was soon bringing in BMW owners from all over southern England. This in turn helped create new business in the showrooms and by 1980 Hughenden was ready to convert to a solus franchise. In Britain only about 15 per cent of all motor cycle dealers operate a solus franchise and Hughenden M40 is one of only a handful of exclusively BMW bike dealerships in the world. Even in Germany only 13 of BMW's 326 bike dealers are exclusive franchises, although about a half combine four- and two-wheel sales.

Hughenden M40 is an 'A' class dealership and stocks the full BMW range of motor cycles. Its exclusive sales territory stretches over 400 square miles (1,000 km^2) of Oxfordshire and Buckinghamshire but it is nationally known because of its regular advertising and its racing sponsorship. It has demonstrator bikes always available for test rides by potential customers and it has an exceptionally well-equipped and organised workshop for service, crash repairs and warranty work. Sales, workshop and spares are run on a monthly profit and loss accountability and all work to established targets. Ron Slater, who worked a professional apprenticeship selling cars, has created a very clear policy of service to the customer. This sees the BMW owner as an asset who will mature and have changing needs leading to a succession of further orders. The secret of selling is seen as encouraging this to happen regularly so that satisfaction from the purchase of the bike leads naturally to accessories, clothing, regular servicing and eventually to bike replacement again. Customer satisfaction is also recognised as being contagious and something that needs to be promoted because it will so often lead to contact with fresh customers won over by the reputation.

It is a keystone of BMW marketing policy that they sell only through their own sales organisation. Indeed, it is estimated that world-wide over 90 per cent of the total BMW output is sold 'in the family'. This means that, unlike some world manufacturers, BMW does not have any substantial problem with unofficial or pirate dealerships. Answerable neither to the company nor the importers, such dealers can seek quick profits by heavy discounting and cutting corners on services to the customer. If allowed to run completely unchecked such operations can pose serious threats to the organised sales outlets which are obliged, as part of their agreements, to maintain certain standards and commitments. In the USA, Capital Cycle Corp have almost made Washington rather than New Jersey the major centre of BMW activity, by supplying genuine parts at 20 per cent off the normal dealers' prices. In Britain the most fascinating 'pirate' has to be Frank Cox of Markhouse Motor Cycles in East London. Frank has a fervent admiration for the traditional values of BMW and his shop is a treasure house of BMW rarities. His customers come from the other side of the world in search of missing bits. His showroom line up all left the BMW factory when it was in Munich, not Berlin. Top of his range is not the 200 km/h R100RS of 1981 but the 100 km/h R52 of 1929. It is here that not only can parts for an R69 be found, but it might even be possible to buy a complete machine. Behind the scenes there is not the electronic test equipment and official tool boards of the official BMW dealers, but the intuitive spannerwork of a mechanic who respects and knows the engines. Frank Cox has been in the business of repairing and renovating old BMWs since 1958 and remains fiercely independent of the importers, buying his parts directly from sources in Germany. His knowledge of the marque is detailed and he is an automatic point of call for owners of the rarer BMW motor cycles who need advice, spares or just a talk about the old days.

In Britain the dealers' work peaks in the spring and around the start of the annual registration period in August. Quiet times for motor cycle sales are in early July and December. In Germany, where motor cycling is a summer time activity, the peak sales are in June and 50 per cent of the annual turnover occurs in the period between March and July.

The average monthly pattern of BMW sales in Britain

Jan	*Feb*	*Mar*	*Apr*	*May*	*Jun*	*Jul*	*Aug*	*Sep*	*Oct*	*Nov*	*Dec*
7%	6%	9%	10%	10%	10%	6%	15%	9%	8%	7%	3%

The Stroke 5 series launched in 1969. After 1972 it featured even more chromium plating. Though fitted with electric start it still retained the familiar kick-start at the side (BMW).

Buyers use their nearest dealer for convenience although they can be attracted from further afield by special offers or a reputation for efficient servicing. Ongar Motor Cycles in Essex and the Carnell Motor Group in Doncaster have extended their spheres of influence by active promotional selling and Gus Kuhn and Hughenden M40 are widely respected for the excellence of their workshops. The scope for independent marketing is rather limited by the control of the importers on supplies, but there still exists some opportunity for the virtuosos to ignore team orders. Although they would concede that BMW has the best strategic view of the motor cycle market some dealers clearly feel that they know their patch and their business best.

New bikes arrive at the dealers packed and sealed as they left the factory in Berlin. They will have travelled to Britain by container lorry through Hamburg to Harwich. They are warehoused in a large countryside depot near Thame in Buckinghamshire. From there they are directed by BMW (GB) in accordance with dealers' targets and orders. Apart from fixing wing mirrors, adding the screen, charging the battery and filling the tank, a BMW motor cycle will run straight out of its packing case. Before the customer collects the bike the dealer carries out a pre-delivery inspection and fits any accessories which have been ordered, such as panniers or crash bars. Pride in ownership of a BMW motor cycle makes the collecting customer particularly fastidious about finish and presentation and it is important for dealers to pay special attention to this key stage in the sale. It is also useful for the dealer to be available at the 'handing over ceremony' to advise first-time owners of the BMWs' unique handling characteristics. First time out on such a motor cycle it is very easy to approach bends too fast because of the smooth and quiet engine noise and novices might experience rear wheel locking if they change down for braking at corners.

Pre-delivery inspection

Dewax, check outer condition of the machine.
Remove battery and charge.
Check oil levels in engine, transmission, rear wheel drive and drive shaft housing.
Check tightness of axle nuts and clamps front and rear.
Check engine mounting bolts, front and rear and centre stand retaining bolts.

Check hose clamps on telescopic forks, carburettors and between drive shaft and transmission.
Tighten rocker arm cover, finned exhaust pipe nut, rear shock absorber mounting, exhaust mounting brackets and fuel petcocks.
Check bolts securing drive shaft at gearbox output flange.
Check fluid level in brake reservoir.
Check oil level in front forks.
Remove float bowls from carburettors and clean. Check operation of floats and needles.
Refit battery. Check operation of: headlight high and low beam, parking light, stop light, turn signals, indicator lights and horn.
Adjust valve clearances.
Check ignition timing.
Check tightness of timing cover to engine.
Test drive and check operation of: clutch, gear change, speedo, steering, brakes. Afterwards inspect for leaks from: engine, gearbox, swinging arm final drive, front forks.
Check for fuel system leaks. Adjust balance for correct idling.
Check took kit, first aid kit and vehicle handbook.

After 600 miles (1,000 km) a new BMW is returned for its first service. This is invariably to the dealer from which is was purchased, although the entire BMW dealer network should be available to the owner. It is not often publicised in Britain, but in North America, where long distance touring is a cult activity, a number of dealers advertise special courtesy facilities for out-of-town riders. This first service does not involve labour charges and the customer pays only for oil, filters and gaskets.

First service details

Change engine oil, replace filter, renew sealing rings and clean oil pan.
Lubricate rear wheel swinging arm bearings.
Lubricate brake and clutch levers and throttle assembly.
Check battery acid level.
Change: transmission oil, drive shaft housing oil, rear wheel drive oil.
Clean air filter.
Check and adjust front fork and wheel bearings.
Adjust brakes and clutch.
Clean and adjust carburettors, adjust throttle cable and clean petcock filter.
Check spark plug gap and ignition timing.
Tighten cylinder head nuts (40 ± 2Nm) then adjust valve clearances.
Tighten all nuts and clamps.
Carry out road test and final inspection.

From now on the service programme calls for regular routine servicing and inspection work every 5,000 miles (7,500 km). The more comprehensive inspection is designed to take place every 10,000 miles (15,000 km), although it is a recommendation that a bike should have a minimum of two services a year even if the distances specified in the rider's manual have not been covered. In some cases fair-weather riders may average less than 2,000 miles a year on their BMWs and for them maintenance checks should be carried out on a time basis.

5,000-mile service* and 10,000 mile inspection

Change engine oil, replace oil filter and renew sealing rings*.
Grease rear swinging arm bearings and check play.
Grease brake and clutch levers, throttle grip, duck oil spray to switchgear*.
Check battery acid level and top up if required*.
Check all oil levels*.
Change transmission oil, drive shaft housing oil, rear wheel drive oil, front fork oil.
Renew air filter. Cleaned at 5,000 miles*.
Check steering head play and adjust if required*.
Check wheel bearing play and adjust if required.
Adjust clutch*.
Adjust brake travel, thickness of pads and renew if required*. Check complete brake system.
Check and adjust carburettors*. Idle speed about 950 rpm.
Renew plugs. Checked at 5,000 miles*.
Check ignition system*.
Check cylinder head nuts and valve clearances*.
Tighten all nuts and clamps*. Inspect alloy wheels.
Road test and final inspection*.

Within the 12 months' warranty period it is vital to comply with the recommended service intervals and to use only genuine BMW parts in order not to invalidate any possible claim on the manufacturer.

Although a BMW motor cycle motors freely and easily from the moment it is ridden from the dealers, it is important to follow recommended running-in rules to ensure that the machine will always subsequently give of its best. BMW suggest that the engine speed is limited to 4,000 rpm for the first 600 miles gradually increasing to 4,500 rpm over the next 600 miles. For the first 300 miles owners should also avoid violent braking so that the tyres and brake pads can bed in properly. A bonus for newcomers to the BMW range is that these machines, like wine, improve with age and may not be considered fully run-in until after their first 5,000 mile service. Although not an officially-adopted procedure, BMW engineers consider that running-in can be helped by occasional short, sharp bursts over 5,000 rpm to prevent carbon build up and to excite oil flow. The important thing to avoid is labouring the engine at low speeds. Properly run-in and regularly serviced the normal BMW engine will comfortably complete 75,000 miles (120,000 km) without major surgery, and many owners have had the experience, with their bikes, of starting the distance recorder from zero again.

BMW prefers that all servicing of its motor cycles are carried out only by staff who have attended their three-day mechanics' courses at their technical training centres. Stripping and repairing of major components such as engines and transmissions should only be done by approved mechanics who have gone on to complete the more advanced technicians' course. In practice dealers vary in the extent to which they observe all the standards specified by BMW for staff training and specialist workshop equipment. Clearly this is a matter which dealers and the importing companies must eventually resolve as owners of expensive machinery such as BMW motor cycles have a right to expect that servicing follows recommended practice in every respect, and that their bikes will be kept in peak condition with a minimum off-road time.

In general the BMW motor cycle range does not involve especially sophisticated maintenance and each bike is relatively easy to service. Indeed, although the *Riders' Handbook* frequently specifies the need for adjustments and repairs to be carried out only by authorised dealers, many owners find they are able to do their own servicing. BMW recognise this by providing a detailed handbook with information about basic service requirements, one of the most comprehensive tool kits supplied by any world manufacturer and by selling genuine service kits for DIY maintenance. The company does, of course, prefer that all its dealers provide a total service to owners and not just concentrate on creaming profits from the sales of new machines. The after-sales side of a dealership is important for customer satisfaction and inadequate servicing not only harms the reputation of the marque, but can lead to unnecessary warranty claims which routine checks might have prevented. At the minimum level it involves dealers being prepared to release their staff for regular training and updating and maintaining the full specialist tool board for BMW machines. It can extend to running an advanced technology workshop equipped with such items as electronic testing rigs to check engine performance, mercury flow gauges for accurately balancing twin carburettors, a motor cycle rolling road for high-performance fault finding, an on-the-bike wheel balancer and proper facilities for rectifying paintwork faults. Very few dealers are equipped to deal properly with paint jobs and most BMW spray work is carried out in Britain by Dream Machine of Nottingham, the specialist firm.

Dealers see the best and the worst of BMW motor cycles. Behind the plate glass of the showrooms the new models gleam in polished splendour. But in the workshops the mechanics see another view of the *meister-maschine* stripped for service or repair. Like anything mechanical even BMWs can go sick and the quality control system which totally eliminates the occasional rogue component has not yet been perfected, particularly for something as complex as a powerful motor cycle. Complaints about any bike are notoriously difficult to compare because riders have such widely different expectations of their machines. What is shoddy workmanship or a serious criticism to one rider passes as a minor paint blemish or an occasionally irritating engine vibration to another. Publicly BMW clearly consider their motor cycles are perfect, and buyers will rarely complain outside the circle of ownership. There is also plenty of evidence from published road tests and the reports of independent consumer surveys by organisations such as the German *Stiftung Warentest* to confirm BMW's leading all-round reliability. Yet any balanced judgement of the Bavarian twins must include warts as well, if only to frustrate their critics. A simple catalogue of faults seen by mechanics would not serve because of the problems of weighing what should be put down to fair wear and tear, what was due to inadequate servicing and what might be explained by the kind of riding abuse the bike had received. Even an analysis of warranty claims amongst BMW owners would have to take into consideration whether the bike had been used habitually in cold, wet Britain or the sunny climes of California. Perhaps the reader will settle for a list of the weak points which the owner of a Stroke 5 model might have reported to mechanics since it first took to the roads. Thirteen years on a Stroke 5 is, in BMW terms, approaching veteran status and an owner might so far have complained about:

Engine and transmission

Oil mist seepage at the base of the cylinder heads and around the push rod seals. Oil filter collapse. Rear crankshaft oil seal failure. Ruptured drive shaft boot. Selector spring breaking. Sticking clutch cable. Excessive play at the input shaft, requiring the gearbox to be shimmed. Erratic idling and sensitive throttle balance with the Bing CV carburettors.

Frame and brakes

Play in head races causing steering wobble. White line weave caused by worn rear tyre. Front fork clonk. Centre stand collapse.

Finish

Some orange peeling. Rust, especially along the seams of silencers. Underpowered battery leading to starting problems. Sporadic flashing interval with indicators.

Dealers rely on the importing company to play a substantial part in supporting their front line activities. These range from basics such as organising an efficient stock ordering and supply system to specific assistance in upgrading premises to match corporate standards. Operating a BMW franchise means striking a balance between profit and security and the loss of independence which can result from over-commitment to the importing company. A dealer could easily feel intimidated by the slick professionalism of the importing company where that looks like taking over control of the whole business. For their part the importing companies want to see dealers acting in the most commercial way. An arena for creating the right sort of liaison is provided by the dealers' council idea and BMW (GB) has been quick to use this approach. The idea, adopted from the car trade, brings dealers and importers together to ensure agreement on common policies. The dealer council meetings make it possible to present revisions to the range, new procedures and generally discuss any issues raised by trying to sell BMW motor cycles. Local dealer councils report to annual meetings which the board of BMW (GB) attend. This form of consultation gives dealers some sense of democratic involvement in company policy and furthers the idea of partnership. A possible area of discussion might be the current rate of warranty claims on the bikes. BMW take pride in the generosity of their warranty operation and their customers are often given the benefit of the doubt when components fail, even after the official period of warranty is finished. However, warranty can be abused by both dealers and customers. Dealers can try to use warranty where the problem is due to faulty servicing or storage deterioration, while the customer can lean on the dealer to keep a machine in an 'as new' condition at BMW's expense. Any lowering of warranty standards would be unwelcome but clearly misuse cannot be left unchecked. Through the medium of the dealers' council the issues can be explored and the sensible compromise achieved.

Inevitably, BMW retain the overall right to run the business in the way it thinks best, but the idea of consultation does remind Munich, the importers and the dealers that they are all on the same side and mutually responsible for the continuing success of the marque. The fact that the organisation is small and close-knit makes this sort of co-operation practicable.

For the customer a realistic and fair dealer/importer agreement must also mean reliable and reasonable treatment from the showrooms. Model availability is likely to be right, warranty matters reach a speedy settlement, parts and accessories meet real consumer needs and loyalty is cemented through consistent and committed service. A motor cycle dealership is a small scale specialist operation and customers are comforted to know that behind it there is strength in depth. This back-up must not, however, become remote, arbitrary and standardised, with management technique losing its human face. For example, it is not the biker's way to be over-impressed by rigidly targetted workshops with set times for each job which can lead to replacement rather than repair or cumbersome re-booking when jobs take longer than planned. Perhaps the consultative relationship between dealer and importer ought to be extended to include customers as well!

12

Tomorrow's BMW

Rapid change and uncertainty are a continuing feature of the 20th century lifestyle and it is not easy to be confident about what the future is likely to bring. Yet with a company such as BMW, which is so aware of its roots and long tradition, the possibilities are perhaps more predictable. This closing chapter explores likely trends in the unfinished story of BMW motor cycles. There are no startling revelations because, in these highly competitive times, companies do not readily divulge their development secrets, nor is a book topical enough to carry too much hearsay or rumour which could already be outdated by the time it is being read. This book has been written from the start as a tribute to BMW and it is not now about to deal in exposé or guesses. Instead it seeks to reassure the reader, who will probably already be an admirer, that the story for motor cycles has no foreseeable ending. The future looks as positive as it has ever looked and what Max Friz set rolling 60 years ago has plenty of life left in it. Those who love good motor cycles need have no fear that the choice of machine in the future will exclude BMW performance and reliability.

Eberhard von Kuenheim, chairman of the board of the Bayerische Motoren Werke AG, 1970 (BMW).

The market for motor cycles is still growing and all the signs from Munich indicate that BMW wishes to continue to grow with it. The cars will obviously remain the dominant side of the business, but investment and building in Spandau will make it possible to double motor cycle production levels over the next decade. Not that BMW will ever turn to mass-production and try to compete in the small bike market. Even with its planned investment programme BMW's motor cycle production is tiny against the volume output of the Japanese makers. The costs of tooling up for a new model require massive sales and the company's exclusive production methods are incapable of supporting the rapid fashion changes which are a feature of the small bike world. It would need a very special set of circumstances to see the BMW badge on a quarter-litre model again. A significant part of BMW's reputation comes from the fact of its production in Germany and it seems unlikely that the company would ever manufacture overseas. Just possible might be an overseas assembling plant in a country such as Brazil where importers face special difficulties yet sales potential is high. Over the past decade BMW has become an international company and it is reasonable to suppose that it will continue to buy into overseas concessions so that it can more directly control its own sales organisation.

The BMW image is now so firmly established in the world of motoring that it must be assumed that production will maintain the reputation for deep-down technical reliability and quality. The research and development division enjoys exceptional support within the company because experience has shown the enormous benefits that

The 1981 R65LS (BMW).

come from re-investing profits in the future. In 1981 some 4 per cent of the total sales income was budgetted for research and development, which amounts to some £75 million. On the motor cycle side some of this investment will undoubtedly go towards improving the performance, the outstanding service life and the reliability of the orthodox boxer twins. Although the Bavarian twins have passed through 60 years of refinement and development, BMW still see a future for them. However, the second half of the '80s should see them joined by a new generation of motor cycles designed to extend and complement BMW's range.

For the twins the future will mean changes in the production methods to take advantage of new materials and more efficient assembly procedures. This is likely to lead to greater use of die casting in lightweight alloys, more use of coloured fibre-glass reinforced plastic and the fitting of fail-safe sealed units similar to the Nivomat suspension. There will also be more widespread use of black box technology to control, measure and record motor cycle functions. Traditionally, BMW have shown a preference on their bikes for technical simplicity rather than complex gadgetry, but once a system has been proved dependable there is no reluctance to adopt it. They seemed slow at the time with electronic ignition, but this system is now of very reliable quality. BMW cars already lead the world in the application of micro-processors and it seems very likely that this experience will quickly lead to numerous bike applications in fuel injection, functional checks and digital displays. Such developments would be politically and environmentally sound, leading to motor cycles with improved fuel consumption, safer anti-locking brakes and vastly improved rider information about the state of machine efficiency and the need for service.

Improved performance for BMWs will continue to come from weight-shedding and improvements to the bikes' aerodynamics. Five years' experience with the RS fairing has already shown how road-holding and performance can be improved by a proper attention to airflow at the design stage of a machine. The recently introduced R65LS has a carefully designed cockpit spoiler which is said to reduce front-wheel lift by a third and makes a major contribution to riding stability. This model also demonstrates some of the weight-saving potential of new materials. Its aluminium compound wheels, jointly developed by BMW and Alusuisse, save 2 kg over the previous model despite using a larger rim opening on the front wheel to improve handling. It also features increased use of moulded plastic fittings, which save weight and offer interesting styling possibilities. The use of matt black chrome finish on two recent models may point to improvements in an area which has been a point of criticism for some time. A breakthrough in silencer design which did not discolour and which reduced emission noises would be a bonus for the boxer twins in meeting proposed new legislation governing noise limits on motor cycles. Other developments seem likely with tyres and suspensions. BMW are still being cautious about tubeless tyres, although other major manufacturers have gone ahead with their use. The bigger Japanese bikes also feature infinitely variable air forks with anti-dive characteristics, although BMW may see its priority as developing the mono-shock rear suspension which works so well on the R80 G/S.

Put together the improvement potential for the boxer twins would be considerable, despite present claims to be near perfection. Obviously, anything which lasts as long as the classical BMW bike designs must have an exciting future too. One design study commissioned by BMW in the summer of 1979 has, appropriately for this chapter, been labelled the Futuro. This advanced motor cycle project was developed not by a bike designer but by sports car specialist Rainer Buchmann of b&b design, Frankfurt. It is seen as the possible shape of things for the boxer concept in the 1990s. The design team were helped by many suggestions from road safety, engine, chassis and construction and use specialists as well as the pure stylists.

The result is a fully-enclosed and streamlined machine with very low frontal area which has a substantially reduced drag coefficient compared with present motor cycles. A comparatively small turbo-charged 800 cc engine gives 75 bhp and can project the bike to speeds of up to 130 mph (210 km/h). The use of a turbocharger with an electronic fuel injection system boosts power output and gives smooth running at all speeds with low fuel consumption. This is also helped by the low, 180 kg, weight of the Futuro. This low weight has been achieved by extensive use of aluminium in the frame, rear swinging arm, brakes and wheels, and light, carbon-fibre reinforced plastic for the fairing. A lengthened wheelbase and the use of car-type universal joints all but eliminates the typical driving torque reactions of a normal BMW twin. Sintered friction pads and an integral braking system, linking both front and rear brakes, ensures that the machine will stop quickly and well even in wet conditions. The most futuristic aspect of the design is within the stream-lined cockpit. Here micro-processor-controlled displays indicate not only engine revs, road speed, oil temperature, oil pressure, turbo boost, battery voltage and time but also provide functional checks on fuel consumption, elapsed time of journey, average speed and even when an oil change or service is due.

Safety features on the Futuro include a clever adaptation of the cockpit, fuel tank and knee recesses to form a single plane which would guide the rider up and clear of the machine in the event of a head-on collision. In-board equipment includes a two-way radio system with electronic signal searching and the ability automatically to over-ride the music and give priority instructions about engine conditions using voice synthesizers. Amplification is by a combination of loudspeakers fitted in the Kevlar-reinforced plastic safety cell coupled with helmet headphones. Luggage

The Futuro with and without its moulded body skin (BMW).

compartments are fitted into the fairing above the rear wheel. Whether, of course, the radical streamlining and integral riding position would be acceptable remains to be determined by road tests in the future. The design does, however, incorporate many features of development which are known to be in the pipelines around the world. Safety, protection from the elements and the cost and performance advantages of good aerodynamics might, of course, persuade bikers that a 'single track car' such as the Futuro, is the shape of things to come.

The closeness of the Futuro Study to the original Max Friz concept of a boxer engine and shaft drive underlines the faith that BMW still have in this form of motor cycling. This company is unique amongst bike manufacturers in remaining so constant for so long to an original engineering idea. Some critics have claimed that this faithfulness to the classical design has outlived its usefulness and the competition now calls for an entirely new concept. This view has gained support with the news that BMW are well-advanced with the development of a multicylinder machine of advanced technical design. Unconventionally for BMW the new bike will be a four-cylinder in-line engine with double overhead camshafts, fuel injection and shaft drive. Water-cooling will be used to ensure even quieter running and the rear suspension will use the monolever system pioneered by the 80 G/S. The 1,000 cc road machine, code named K589, will become the BMW flagship in the mid-'80s. Its arrival will not be before time for dealers anxiously watching the emergence of technically-advanced turbo machines from the Japanese factories and wondering whether the traditional push-rod twins could continue to compete. The launching of a BMW four will also realise a rumour which has cropped up at least twice during the long reign of the flat twins. Back in 1931 Munich was said to be preparing a four-cylinder record-breaker for Ernst Henne and there were strong rumours in the mid-'60s that a BMW four was under development.

With BMW now really switched on to marketing it seems likely that the motor cycle side of the business will continue to follow trends set by the car division. If the expansion at Spandau does double output, sales targets for motor cycles will be significantly increased. This might create problems of exclusivity when the 'discerning few' becomes a multitude. The recent selling activity has put many new BMW bikes on the road and some would hold to the view that a market such as

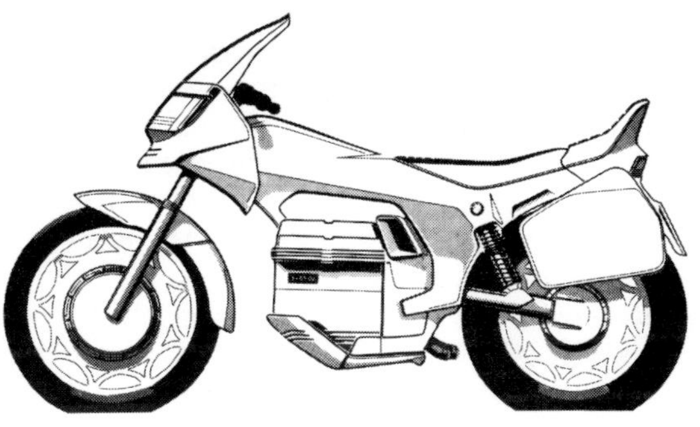

BMW Touring Module

BMW Moduro

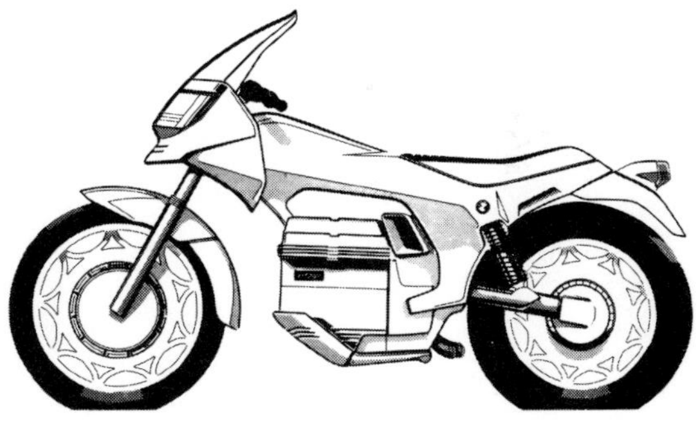

BMW Corsa Module

Modular design studies in the dreams of BMW R&D engineers (BMW).

Britain is already close to saturation point for big, quality motor cycles. There is some risk that the difference which once made all the difference could be eroded away. BMW owners are used to the idea that their bikes do not become obsolete and that their high resale value makes them almost an investment. These selling points might lose their value if rapid model changes, special offers to clear old stocks or any loss of confidence in the twins occurs.

The arrival of the R80 G/S and the R65LS have gone some way to prepare the buffs for a different look, but styling for the new generation bikes does create something of a dilemma. Sixty years of slowly refining the boxer concept has left a BMW motor cycle easily identifiable, but the new models involve a radical departure. This question of brand identity has been resolved on the BMW cars by retaining the traditional kidney-shaped radiator grill even on such exotica as the M1. For the bikes it will be less easy to identify a BMW once the flat-twin layout has been altered. Presumably, the scene is being set for a re-run of the last upheaval when the Stroke series appeared. Traditionalists will stay with the boxer models changing slowly and reluctantly only as replacements become unobtainable. If the past is any criterion this could mean the flat twins running about well into the next century. Many of the 1950s models are still going strong and refusing to wear out 30 years on. The other BMW motor cycle owner will be into the high technology machines and will want to change bikes frequently to keep up to date with the latest developments. Such an owner will take pride in a machine which advanced engineering has made safer, smarter and more efficient than ever before. It will be this desire to ride the latest model which will provide the necessary regular volume sales. The company will then have succeeded in creating a bike market that closely parallels the way its car sales have developed. Some dealers have already separated their volume sales from the up-market end by creating superbike centres. It may be that as the new generation of high technology bikes arrive on the scene there will be an increase in specialist solus dealers able to handle fast-changing developments in motor cycle design and owners changing models at frequent and planned intervals. The luxury motor cycle dealership will have arrived.

The future for BMW motor cycles looks set for a period of interesting challenge and change. Motor cycling has never been universally popular or acceptable and it has been no mean achievement for BMW to have persevered with its small-scale, hand-crafted form of production for 60 years through world crises, financial difficulties and increasingly tough competition from the mass-market factories. What now seems fascinating is that BMW, independent as ever, plans to take the fight to the opposition by carving out a completely fresh image, free of tradition and heritage, and unashamedly commited to the new technology. Through its sales reorganisation it has created leaner and fitter importing companies and dealer networks capable of accepting the challenge and now it only needs to deliver the goods. So long as the formula proves to be right BMW's new generation models should do for bikes in the '80s what the 1500 saloon did for cars in the '60s.

Appendix

A Diamond Jubilee of models

Model	***Helios***	***R32***	***R37***	***R39***	***R42***	***R47***
Engine type	M2B15	M2B33 sv	M2B36 ohv	M40 ohv	M43 sv	M51 ohv
Cylinders	2	2	2	1	2	2
Bore × stroke (mm)	68 × 68	68 × 68	68 × 68	68 × 68	68 × 68	68 × 68
Displacement (cc)	494	494	494	247	494	494
Compression ratio	5:1	5:1	6.2:1	6:1	4.9:1	5.8:1
Claimed output bhp	6.5	8.5	16	6.5	12	18
rpm	2,800	3,300	4,000	4,000	3,400	4,000
Gears	3	3	3	3	3	3
Fuel tank (litres)	Not available	14	14	10	14	14
Weight (kg)	Not available	120	134	110	126	130
Top speed (km/h)	Not available	95	115	100	95	110
*Fuel consumption**	3	3.5	4	2.5	3	4.5
Years of production	1921/23	1923-6	1925-6	1925-7	1926-8	1927-8
Quantity built	Not available	3,100	175	1,000	6,900	1,700
Price (RM)	Not available	2,200	2,900	1,870	1,510	1,850

Model	***R52***	***R57***	***R62***	***R63***	***R11***	***R16***
Engine type	M57 sv	M59 ohv	M56S1 sv	M60S1 ohv	M56 sv	M60 ohv
Cylinders	2	2	2	2	2	2
Bore × stroke (mm)	78 × 63	68 × 68	78 × 78	83 × 68	78 × 78	83 × 68
Displacement (cc)	487	492	745	734	740	730
Compression ratio	5:1	5.8:1	5.5:1	6.2:1	5.5:1	6.5:1
Claimed output bhp	12	18	18	24	18	25
rpm	3,400	4,000	3,400	4,000	3,400	4,000
Gears	3	3	3	3	3	3
Fuel tank (litres)	12.5	12.5	12.5	12.5	14	14
Weight (kg)	152	150	155	155	162	165
Top speed (km/h)	100	115	115	115	100	120
*Fuel consumption**	3.5	3.5	5	5	3.5	5
Years of production	1928-29	1928-30	1928-29	1928-29	1929-34	1929-34
Quantity built	9,000	1,000	4,000	1,000	8,300	1,900
Price (RM)	1,510	1,700	1,450	1,750	1,630	2,040
£ in Britain	98 (1931)	115 (1931)	110 (1931)	126 (1931)	110 (1931)	120 (1931)

Model	***R2***	***R4***	***R12***	***R17***	***R3***	***R5***
Engine type	M67S1 ohv	M69S1 ohv	M56S6 sv	M60S4 ohv	203/1	254/1
Cylinders	1	1	2	2	1	2
Bore × stroke (mm)	63 × 64	78 × 84	78 × 78	83 × 68	68 × 84	68 × 68
Displacement (cc)	198	398	745	736	305	494
Compression ratio	6.7:1	5.7:1	5.2:1	6.5:1	6:1	6.7:1
Claimed output bhp	6	12	18	33	11	24
rpm	3,500	3,500	3,400	5,000	4,200	5,800
Gears	3	3/4	4	4	4	4
Fuel tank (litres)	11	12	14	14	12.5	15
Weight (kg)	110	137	185	183	149	165
Top speed (km/h)	95	100	110	140	100	140
*Fuel consumption**	2.8	3.5	5.4	5	3	3.5
Years of production	1931-6	1932-8	1935-8	1935-7	1936	1936-7
Quantity built	15,300	15,200	36,000	450	750	2,600
Price (RM)	975	1,150	1,630	2,040	995	1,550
£ in Britain	70 (1936)	85 (1938)	115 (1937)	125 (1937)	77 (1937)	115 (1937)

Model	***R20***	***R35***	***R6***	***R23***	***R51***	***R61***
Engine type	220/1	235/1	261/1 sv	223/1	254/1	261/1 sv
Cylinders	1	1	2	1	2	2
Bore × stroke (mm)	60 × 68	72 × 84	70 × 78	68 × 68	68 × 68	70 × 78
Displacement (cc)	192	340	596	247	494	596
Compression ratio	6:1	6:1	6:1	6:1	6.7:1	5.7:1
Claimed output bhp	8	14	18	10	24	18
rpm	5,400	4,500	4,800	5,400	5,600	4,800
Gears	3	4	4	3	4	4
Fuel tank (litres)	12	12	15	9.6	14	14
Weight (kg)	130	155	175	135	182	184
Top speed (km/h)	95	100	125	90	140	115
*Fuel consumption**	2.5	3	3.5	3	4	4
Years of production	1937-8	1937-40	1937	1938-41	1938-40	1938-41
Quantity built	5,000	15,387	1,850	8,000	13,000	4,300
Price (RM)	725	995	1,375	750	1,595	1,420
£ in Britain	65 (1938)	85 (1938)	110 (1938)	59 (1938)	123 (1938)	118 (1938)

Model	***R66***	***R71***	***R75***	***R24***	***R25***	***R51/2***
Engine type	266/1	271/1 sv	275/2	224/1	224/2	254/1
Cylinders	2	2	2	1	1	2
Bore × stroke (mm)	69.8 × 78	78 × 78	78 × 78	68 × 68	68 × 68	68 × 68
Displacement (cc)	597	745	745	247	245	494
Compression ratio	6.8:1	5.5:1	5.6:1	6.75:1	6.5:1	6.3:1
Claimed output bhp	30	22	26	12	12	24
rpm	5,300	4,600	4,000	5,600	5,600	5,800
Gears	4	4	10	4	4	4
Fuel tank (litres)	14	14	24	12	12	14
Weight (kg)	187	187	420	130	140	185
Top speed (km/h)	145	125	95	95	95	140
*Fuel consumption**	4.5	4.5	6.3	3.5	3.5	4
Years of production	1938-41	1938-41	1941-4	1949	1950	1950
Quantity built	2,000	3,500	16,500	12,010	23,405	5,050
Price (DM)	1,695	1,595	Not available	1,750	1,750	2,750
£ in Britain	130 (1938)	123 (1938)	Not available	Not available	Not available	Not available

Model	***R51/3***	***R25/2***	***R67***	***R68***	***R25/3***	***R26***
Engine type	252/1	224/2	267/1	268/1	252/1	224/5
Cylinders	2	1	2	2	1	1
Bore × stroke (mm)	68 × 68	68 × 68	72 × 73	72 × 73	68 × 68	68 × 68
Displacement (cc)	490	245	590	590	245	245
Compression ratio	6.3:1	6.4:1	5.6:1	7.6:1	7:1	7.5:1
Claimed output bhp	24	12	26	35	13	15
rpm	5,800	5,800	5,500	7,000	5,800	6,400
Gears	4	4	4	4	4	4
Fuel tank (litres)	17	17	17	17	12	15
Weight (kg)	190	142	192	193	150	158
Top speed (km/h)	140	100	145	160	119	128
*Fuel consumption**	4.5	4.5	4.6	4.6	2.9	3.3
Years of production	1951-4	1951-3	1952-4	1953-5	1955-60	1955-60
Quantity built	18,425	38,651	5,730	1,453	47,700	30,238
Price (DM)	3,000	1,990	2,875	3,950	2,060	2,150
£ in Britain	427 (1951)	276 (1951)	452 (1951)	600 (1951)	228 (1956)	256 (1956)

Model	***R50***	***R69***	***R60***	***R27***	***R50S***	***R69S***
Engine type	252/2	268/2	267/4	226/2	252/3	268/3
Cylinders	2	2	2	1	2	2
Bore × stroke (mm)	68 × 68	72 × 73	72 × 73	68 × 68	68 × 68	72 × 73
Displacement (cc)	490	590	590	245	490	590
Compression ratio	6.8:1	8:1	6.5:1	8.2:1	9.2:1	9.5:1
Claimed output bhp	26	35	28	18	35	42
rpm	5,800	6,800	5,600	7,400	7,650	7,000
Gears	4	4	4	4	4	4
Fuel tank (litres)	17	17	17	15	17	17
Weight (kg)	195	202	195	162	198	202
Top speed (km/h)	140	165	145	130	160	175
*Fuel consumption**	4.5	4.6	4.2	3.9	5.1	5.3
Years of production	1955-60	1955-60	1956-67	1960-7	1960-2	1960-9
Quantity built	32,532	2,819	20,828	15,364	1,634	11,417
Price (DM)	3,050	3,950	3,235	2,430	3,535	4,030
£ in Britain	378 (1956)	492 (1956)	390 (1957)	330 (1962)	484 (1962)	530 (1962)

Model	***R50/5***	***R60/5***	***R75/5***	***R60/6***	***R75/6***	***R90/6***
Engine type	246	246	246	247	247	247
Cylinders	2	2	2	2	2	2
Bore × stroke (mm)	67 × 70.6	73.5 × 70.6	82 × 70.6	73.5 × 70.6	82 × 70.6	90 × 70.6
Displacement (cc)	494	599	745	599	745	898
Compression ratio	8.6:1	9.2:1	9:1	9.2:1	9:1	9:1
Claimed output bhp	32	40	50	40	50	60
rpm	6,400	6,400	6,500	6,500	6,500	6,500
Gears	4	4	4	5	5	5
Fuel tank (litres)	22	22	22	18	18	18
Weight (kg)	185	190	190	200	200	200
Top speed (km/h)	157	167	175	167	177	188
*Fuel consumption**	4.6	4.8	4.5	5.5	4.5	5
Years of production	1969-73	1969-73	1969-73	1973-6	1973-6	1973-6
Quantity built	8,650	22,721	38,370	13,511	17,587	21,105
Price (DM)	4,295	5,465	5,615	5,745	6,650	7,150
£ in Britain	762 (1970)	826 (1970)	998 (1970)	1,177 (1974)	1,373 (1974)	1,520 (1974)

Model	***R90S***	***R60/7***	***R75/7***	***R100/7***	***R100/S***	***R100RS***
Engine type	247	247/76	247/76	247/76	247/76	247/76
Cylinders	2	2	2	2	2	2
Bore × stroke (mm)	90 × 70.6	73.5 × 70.6	82 × 70.6	94 × 70.6	94 × 70.6	94 × 70.6
Displacement (cc)	898	599	745	980	980	980
Compression ratio	9.5:1	9.2:1	9:1	9:1	9.5:1	9.5:1
Claimed output bhp	67	40	50	60	65	70
rpm	7,000	6,400	6,200	6,500	6,600	7,250
Gears	5	5	5	5	5	5
Fuel tank (litres)	24	24	24	24	24	24
Weight (kg)	205	195	195	195	200	210
Top speed (km/h)	200	167	177	188	200	200
*Fuel consumption**	5	5.5	4.5	4.5	5.3	5.3
Years of production	1973-6	1976-9	1976-9	1976-9	1976-80†	1976-80†
Quantity built	17,464	46,747	61,676	18,826	12,393†	21,557†
Price (DM)	8,510	6,850	7,985	8,590	10,190	11,210
£ in Britain	1,875 (1974)	1,699 (1977)	2,179 (1977)	2,099 (1977)	2,499 (1977)	2,999 (1977)

Model	***R80/7***	***R100RS***	***R100RT***	***R100CS***	***R100***	***R80 G/S***
Engine type	247/76	247/76	247	247	247	247
Cylinders	2	2	2	2	2	2
Bore × stroke (mm)	84.8 × 70.6	94 × 70.6	94 × 70.6	94 × 70.6	94 × 70.6	84.8 × 70.6
Displacement (cc)	798	980	980	980	980	798
Compression ratio	9.2:1	9.5:1	9.5:1	9.5:1	8.2:1	8.2:1
Claimed output bhp	55 (50)**	70	70	70	67	50
rpm	7,000	7,000	7,000	7,000	7,000	6,500
Gears	5	5	5	5	5	5
Fuel tank (litres)	24	24	24	24	24	19.5
Weight (kg)	195	210	217	200	198	167
Top speed (km/h)	180 (170)**	200	190	200	195	168
*Fuel consumption**	4.8 (5)**	5.75	5.75	5.75	5.5	5
Years of production	1976-9	1976-	1979-	1980-	1976-	1980-
Quantity built	14,038	21,557†	10,080†	Not available	12,393†	1,666†
Price (DM) (1981)	Not available	13,490	13,490	10,990	9,990	8,590
£ in Britain	1,899 (1977)	3,497 (1981)	3,497 (1981)	2,795 (1981)	2,594 (1981)	2,449 (1981)
Fr in France	Not available	36,400	34,100	31,000	27,600	25,100
Lir in Italy	Not available	8.39 million	8.5 million	7.18 million	6.28 million	5.5 million

Model	***R65***	***R45***	***R65LS***
Engine type	248	248	248
Cylinders	2	2	2
Bore × stroke (mm)	82 × 61.5	70 × 61.5	82 × 61.5
Displacement (cc)	650	473	650
Compression ratio	9.2:1	9.2:1 (8.2:1)**	9.2:1
Claimed output bhp	50	35 (27)**	50
rpm	7,250	7,250 (6,500)**	7,250
Gears	5	5	5
Fuel tank (litres)	22	22	22
Weight (kg)	185	185	185
Top speed (km/h)	175	160 (145)**	180
*Fuel consumption**	4.6	4.5 (5)**	4.6
Years of production	1978-	1978-	1981-
Quantity built	14,254†	17,488†	Not available
Price (DM)	7,990	6,890	8,590
£ in Britain	2,194 (1981)	1,995 (1981)	2,450 (1981)
Fr in France	22,500	Not available	24,100
Lir in Italy	5 million	3.85 million	5.5 million

*Fuel consumption given in litres/100 km.
†Only to 1980.
**Detuned version.

Index